THE UNTOLD SECRETS OF THE JOB SEARCH

PRACTICAL STRATEGIES TO GIVE YOU AN ADVANTAGE ON YOUR JOB HUNT

Z LAWSON

CONTENTS

Just for you

A FREE GIFT FOR OUR READERS!

A list of 5 common mistakes people make whilst searching for a job and info on how you can overcome them!
Visit this link:

WWW.Z-LAWSON.COM

For further discussion and support, join our community of advisors and friends on

www.facebook.com/groups/jobsearchadviceforum

INTRODUCTION

When you are unemployed, job hunting becomes your full-time job. You wake up early in the morning, prepare a cup of coffee, and prepare yourself for the long day of sending applications ahead. Truth be told, the demands of this job aren't at all demanding; however, they are tiresome. All that is required of you is to access company websites or job portals and submit your generic resume to every job post that seems promising. The process, as most people know, is repetitive and mind-numbing. It starts taking a toll on you when you have submitted your application to numerous recruiters every day for months. You ask yourself, "Am I not qualified enough?" "Is my experience too short?" or "Is this even the right career field for me?"

Job seekers can experience self-doubt and pressure during their job hunt, which can be genuinely damaging for their confidence. The more their confidence is knocked down, the less bold they become in applying for job posts they are qualified to occupy. After months of searching for a job, it's tempting to reduce your expectations and apply for underpaying and underskilled jobs. It's not that you genuinely wanted to be an administration clerk, but the fact that your experience as an accountant is being overlooked, you don't mind settling. As many may have come to know, settling is one of the biggest traps in the job market. Once you settle for a low paying or low qualified job, it becomes challenging to work your way to the salary or position you used to hold.

The golden rule for advancing in the job market is to seek a career and not a job. While many people are more than happy to have a job that provides them with an income, only those who build a career for themselves are always in high demand. To build a career, you would need to place more focus and meaning behind the work you do and always have a goal that you seek to achieve in your mind. In my many years in corporate, I have found that those who successfully climbed the corporate ladder were people who knew what they were climbing towards. Visual learners had a mental picture of the positions they wanted to hold someday, and others preferred writing down a list of milestones and tactics to carry out their goals in the near future.

However, what is undeniable is the amount of intentionality it takes to find a job or work your way up the corporate ladder. If it were so easy to land your dream job, there wouldn't be high unemployment levels, employees resigning or jumping ship to work for a competitor. As a job seeker, you sit in a seat of power, whether you know it or not. The reason why you have so much power right now is because you are a free agent. You don't work for anybody, and therefore, you are less restrained in approaching the ideal company in your industry of choice. This book will expose you to hidden secrets that make the job hunt less strenuous and more advantageous to you being noticed by the right people. It will challenge your perception you have of yourself, your value, and the mindset you hold going into the job market. By the end of reading this book, you will have the ingredients for building a successful career and a structured game plan that will outline the steps you must take moving forward.

The knowledge and nuggets of wisdom I will pass on to you are a culmination of my years of experience in the corporate world and the many lessons I have learned along the way. A long while ago now, I was an undergraduate who had secured internships at major brands each year of my degree. I've helped thousands more secure postgraduate roles after that—in companies including Barclays, Deloitte, Unilever, UBS, GSK, Rolls Royce, NHS, and Civil Service. I was so desperate to secure summer internships and a graduate job straight after university to survive and help my family. After university, I decided to set up a website to help other students and experienced professionals find work opportunities as effortlessly. Since launching my website, I have helped over 3,000 people build careers in 19 countries after going through my training program.

Career coaching and teaching job seekers how to prepare and secure meaningful work have since been a passion of mine. Helping you achieve your ideal job matters deeply to me because what you're about to learn has helped me live the life I have always desired in my mind. I've searched for all kinds of jobs that you can think of, and I understand the pain and frustration involved during the job hunt. I also know that there is a lot of pressure associated with securing an offer. For some, it is family pressure, peer pressure, or even worse—financial pressure. For me, securing a job was the only option I had to pay for my university fees, therefore receiving an offer was a BIG deal! My intention for writing this book is to share my models, strategies, and tips for landing your ideal job and hopefully become your career mentor while you climb each step up the corporate ladder.

THE X-FACTOR

Many job seekers don't hear this often, but I will say it openly: YOU are the X-Factor when seeking a job. When companies interview you, they are, in essence, looking for that value that only you can offer them. I understand how stressful the job hunt can be and how sometimes the pressure causes you to lose your confidence. You start taking your defeats personally and lose sight of the fact that your value has not decreased because another company failed to see it. Job seekers who fail to recognize their own worth will eventually hide it even when they are meant to display it. For instance, you may be modest to let a recruiter know about your previous accomplishments because you don't believe it is relevant or recent enough to mention. Alternatively, you may choose to understate your strengths out of fear of looking arrogant and instead exaggerate your weaknesses because you want to seem relatable.

As you can see, the failure to acknowledge and strategically showcase your value can prove detrimental to your career prospects. As the job market has grown more competitive, companies have begun seeking exceptional candidates to join their world-class teams. Surprisingly, the candidates in high demand are not those who have the highest education or the most impressive work experience. While these factors significantly make the candidate more attractive, it isn't what differentiates one candidate from another. The true differentiator between candidates (which also exposes the candidates' X Factor) was their soft skills. Over 75% of managers are looking for candidates who demonstrate soft skills. This means that candidates who boast about an IQ of 180 are not considered assets if their personalities or attitudes aren't adding value.

Soft skills are a combination of your positive attributes, characteristics, and competencies that can improve your work performance, enhance your relationships with colleagues, and support team productivity. While soft skills may be linked to emotional intelligence, they also include being a good communicator and listener, effectively resolving conflict, forming positive relationships, and collaborating in harmony with others. Recruiters can pick up on these soft skills through your ability to express who you are, what you believe, and the meaning you place behind your work. They may also look for someone who is goal-oriented, shows integrity, and can be held accountable for their work. Therefore, understanding what recruiters are looking for, you can see the emphasis placed on the value that you bring as an individual, apart from your qualifications or previous work experience. You are a valuable asset that companies are looking for!

YOUR SELF-WORTH IS NOT FOUND IN YOUR JOB

The terms "self-worth" and "self-value" are often used interchangeably. To put it simply, individuals with a sense of self-worth tend to see value in themselves and their contributions. The difference between the two words is so minimal that they may be used within similar contexts. To explain the importance of exposing your X-Factor, I will speak in terms of self-worth. According to the Cambridge dictionary, self-worth can be described as "the value you give to your life and achievements." It is the feeling that assures you that you are the right person and deserve to be treated with dignity. Don't be tempted to think of this feeling as being a display of self-confidence because self-confidence is not an overall evaluation of yourself; it is merely being competent in one or more specific areas in your life.

A job seeker doesn't need to maintain a high level of self-confidence in their skills or competencies because it is natural to doubt your capabilities, especially in competitive industries. However, job seekers cannot compromise on their self-worth, which is the self-assessment of their value as a human being as it pertains to their thoughts, feelings, and behaviors about their life. The self-worthy theory offers us an interesting insight into the intention behind most of our efforts as human beings. It states that many of our priorities in life are founded on our subconscious need for self-acceptance. We yearn for that moment where our mind, body, and soul are in alignment, and we feel fulfilled in who we are and how we choose to live our lives. This hidden desire for self-acceptance might also explain the reason behind our search for the perfect job.

Self-acceptance is reached when we feel that we have attained a certain level of achievement or success. Without any tangible achievements, we seek external validation to prove that we are indeed valuable individuals. This is one of the reasons why relatives, friends, and colleagues compete with one another. They are not necessarily competing for the biggest or most expensive car; instead, they compete for the high-status symbol that the car, job, relationship, or promotion would bring, which they associate with their self-worth. The self-worth theory states that through competition with others, people can feel a sense of achievement, making them feel proud of who they are, thus enhancing their self-acceptance.

Take a few moments to reflect on your life growing up in your household or community. Think back to the time you graduated from college or university. During this time, what kind of pressures did you experience related to finding a job? How many of those pressures stemmed from previous assumptions your family or community had about you finding a decent job to carry some of the household responsibility? Regardless of the family background or community in which you grew up, I guarantee that most people who read this book will relate to the societal pressures associated with securing a job. It is understandable why this pressure exists. There has always been a subtle fear or shame tied to being jobless in our society. If you grew up in a poverty-stricken background, you would have seen the example of the uncle who is an alcoholic and is humiliated for his lack of ambition and low-status in the family. On the contrary, if you grew up in a middle-class home, you would have seen firsthand how retrenchments, bankruptcy, and failed businesses can lead to a circulation of rumors and slander within your community.

There has always been a subtle weight of expectation placed on job security and position in the family or the greater community. In many communities, it is implied that to have neither of these is a disappointment and completely unacceptable. Being jobless is seen as a form of failure, low ambition, or sheer laziness. This shame of being unemployed says more about you as an individual than the scarcity of jobs in the economy. In other words, being unemployed lowers a person's sense of self-worth because without any display of achievement, they can't see the value in themselves, nor can their communities see it either. As members of this society, we are constantly pressured and expected to contribute. Most of the time, this contribution is expected to be made through a stable nine-to-five job. An individual is only seen as worthy when they have evidence to show for their worthiness.

As society mistakenly sees it, the X Factor lies in what a person can do instead of who they are. This is an outdated way of thinking, but one that is still perpetuated in our society today. Job seekers have therefore suffered two fatal blows, the first coming from their own disappointment for not being financially secure in their lives, and the second coming from the disappointment felt from their loved ones or community. The truth is that your value does not escape you when you are jobless. Just because you are at home and your spouse or friends are at work, it doesn't mean that you are less of an asset or are less significant in your life. The formula that many incorrectly use is that it takes being successful to become valuable. The inverse is actually the truth. It takes finding your X-Factor or value and effectively demonstrating it to become successful.

REJECTION IS REDIRECTION

For many people, their perspective on rejection is the only thing holding them back from effectively demonstrating their X-Factor. What have you learned about rejection in the past? That it is humiliating, a sign of weakness, or a terrible misfortune? Most of our adopted beliefs regarding rejection are rooted in fear-based justifications. For instance, someone may be afraid of experiencing rejection because they tie it to their self-esteem. When they receive a rejection email, they may interpret it as a sign of their own inadequacy. Therefore, they will fear rejection because of their belief that rejection will expose their weaknesses. The fear of rejection creates self-imposed blockages in your path toward attaining the kind of job you desire. Naturally, when you are fearful of something, you will avoid doing it. Similarly, the fear of being rejected by prospective employers may dissuade job seekers from applying to open job posts in the first place.

Essentially, the fear of rejection is a form of self-sabotage. For instance, your own disempowered beliefs and feelings about the outcome of your job application could restrain you from making the necessary engagement with your future employer. There are many real-life case studies of people who chose to perceive their rejection as redirection. These people didn't come from wealthy backgrounds; however, today, they are among the world's wealthiest people. You may be wondering what it was about their belief system that made them turn hopeless situations into life-producing outcomes. To simply put it, they never questioned their self-worth or their talent even when their communities and business associates disapproved of them.

One of these great men is Jan Koum, the inventor of the most popular app known as WhatsApp. He was born and raised in Ukraine, in a town near Kiev. As a teenage kid, Koum worked as a floor cleaner at a local grocery store to support himself and his mother, who was living off of food stamps and government support at the time. Koum, however, had discovered that he had an interest in technology, and at 18 years old, he taught himself computer networking through studying manuals. His self-taught education on computers had given him enough courage to enroll at San Jose University, where he studied math and computer science. While studying, he decided to work part-time to continue sending money home. He was fortunate enough to land a job as a security tester at Ernst & Young—

this is also where he first met his friend and WhatsApp co-founder, Brian Acton.

After a few years, the duo left Ernst & Young to work at Yahoo! Koum worked as an infrastructure engineer, which offered him an incredible opportunity to learn more about the systems behind one of the world's leading search engines. He decided that it was best to drop out of university to grasp as much knowledge as possible at Yahoo. After nine years of soaking up technical knowledge, he and his friend Acton spontaneously decided to leave their corporate jobs and take a year off to travel and decompress. Their vacation abroad was rudely interrupted by a frightening reality that they were now unemployed. Confident in their years of experience as engineers, they were adamant that they would find a job easily. Both men applied to work at Facebook in 2009, and unfortunately, they were rejected. In August 2009, Brain Acton shared his bitter taste of rejection with his followers on Twitter, writing, "Facebook turned me down. It was a great opportunity to connect with some fantastic people. Looking forward to life's next adventure."

Even though Koum was still living on his $400,000 savings that he earned while at Yahoo, like many other job seekers, he felt the pressure to go back into the job market and earn a living. The only difference between Koum and many other hopefuls looking for work is that Koum knew that he was an asset and would someday become successful with the knowledge he knew about computers and software. He decided that entrepreneurship was the most appropriate route for him because he had so many ideas and plans that the corporate environment would not accommodate. From an early age, Koum had learned how to be a self-starter, a person who is capable and highly motivated to succeed in life without requiring any motivation. With his soft skills underneath his belt, he looked at the technological environment with optimism and waiting for the right opportunity to reveal itself.

This golden opportunity came around in 2009 when Koum decided to purchase an iPhone and realized that its fairly new application, known as the AppStore, was about to unleash an entire industry of new downloadable apps. This sparked an idea in Koum's mind. He thought, "Wouldn't it be cool to build an app with statuses next to people's names? The statuses would show whether a person was on a call, their battery was low, or maybe at the gym." As the months progressed, so did Koum's idea. He was experienced enough to code the backend; however, he needed an iPhone developer to help him refine his app and further customize it. During the planning stages of the app, Koum had already come up with the name WhatsApp. He loved the name because it reminded him of the colloquial term "What's up," which was a catchy name for an instant messaging app.

WhatsApp's launch wasn't as successful as Koum had thought it would be. The earlier versions of the app kept crashing or would randomly get stuck. The turn out of users was also very low. It was mostly a handful of his close friends and family members who had downloaded the app several months after it had launched. As problems related to the app kept piling upon his shoulder, Koum felt discouraged when he told his best friend Acton that he was planning on shutting the app down and looking for a regular job. Acton refused to join Koum in his pity party. Instead, he told him that he would be a fool to quit so far into his journey. He pleaded with Koum to wait a few more months and see what would become of the app.

Another opportunity came when Apple launched push notifications where app developers could ping users when they were not using the app. Koum grabbed this opportunity with both hands and made a few changes to the WhatsApp features. He made updates that allowed a user's friends list to be notified when they changed their status. These notifications were soon used to send instant messages like "How are you doing?" and people would respond to them. As short messages were exchanged back and forth, Koum realized that his app had become a powerful messaging service. People from across the world could communicate with each other instantly. This encouraged him to develop WhatsApp 2.0, which had a messaging component, and suddenly his users grew to 250,000 over a short period of time. Sensing that his app was about to blow up, he contacted his friend Acton who was unemployed at the time and working on another startup idea. They sat together around Acton's kitchen table and planned what would become the beginning of the WhatsApp we know and love today.

WhatsApp became a recognizable brand globally. Its users had superseded those of Blackberry's BBM, Google's G-Talk, and Skype. Its claim to fame sparked the interest of Facebook—the company that had rejected Koum and Acton's application for work. Facebook was interested in purchasing WhatsApp from the duo, and they were willing to pay serious money. In 2014, after a series of talks, Koum and Acton agreed to a $19 billion deal to sell WhatsApp to Facebook. The deal, however, was not signed in a boardroom where many corporate deals are normally handled. Koum had already picked a perfect spot where the deal would be signed. He drove the businessmen a few blocks from the WhatsApp headquarters in Mountain View to an abandoned white building across the train tracks. This white building was the former North County Social Services office where Koum and his mother once stood waiting to collect food stamps. This is where he decided to sign the contract, symbolizing that the series of misfortune and downturns in his life were instrumental in shaping who he became.

THE "BUSINESS DEVELOPMENT STAGE"

Jan Koum's story highlights a fundamental lesson that many job seekers can learn—nothing in your life happens by accident. You may be a student currently sitting at home with your bachelor's degree, wondering when you are going to receive your big break. Before graduating from college, you had your whole life planned out; by 23, you would graduate and find a job immediately, by 24, you would purchase your first car, and by 26, you would have saved enough money to place as a deposit on your first home. However, life had a different plan for you. Even though you would have never chosen to spend your 20s, 30s, or 40s in this kind of predicament, I guarantee you that you are not on this path by accident. Imagine the guilt that Koum felt sitting without a job at home and thinking about the secure job position he left at Yahoo. However, despite Koum's inner critic's voice, he soldiered on and found that his journey had not been a failure.

It is important to carefully consider what you believe is true about yourself and this temporary phase in your life during your unemployment season. When you allow disempowering thoughts to consume you, it won't be easy to see opportunities when they present themselves. Koum never stayed unemployed for too long because he refused to question his capabilities. He believed that he was an asset and that at some point, his skills will become useful. This conviction sheltered his mind from identifying with his momentary low point in life. Similarly to Koum, you are responsible for choosing how you respond to the low points that may present themselves in your environment. You have the power to decide how painful or empowering this season of unemployment will be for you. Those who are willing to continue on the path of self-development through this season and refine their X-Factor will consider this season to be the "Business Development Stage" of their life.

Many of you who have flirted with entrepreneurship will understand what this business development stage entails. However, it is worth explaining this concept by referring to you as the business. Generally, a business matures in five stages. The first stage is the business development stage or seed stage, where its foundations are laid. After, the business grows over a few years to become a startup. Some businesses never outgrow the startup stage, but those that successfully do, move on to the growth or establishment stage. At this point, the business is making millions of dollars per annum, and the directors are enjoying fat checks. Many businesses are comfortable staying at this stage, but the ambitious ones outgrow it and move along to the expansion stage. In this stage, businesses expand their product or service offerings, their geographical reach, or decide to acquire new companies. What follows after the expansion stage is the maturity stage, where businesses have maximized their growth potential and are now given the task to maintain the steady flow of revenue they can generate.

You are a business named Me Inc. Your business is new and has a promising future ahead of it. It is a B2B business that offers other companies exceptional value in the form of the many skills and qualities you come packaged with. While your business is an asset, no one knows about you yet. Thus, your unemployment season becomes your business development stage where you differentiate yourself from other businesses and figure out strategies for growing your influence and reach. The business development stage of a business is always exciting because this is where a founder can be creative in designing a meaningful business brand. Your brand will be the sum of your personality, skills, qualifications, value proposition, and communication strategy. What sustains your brand and effectively allows it to stand out from the rest is its ability to offer your future employer long-term value.

Therefore, your business development stage will consist of three processes that are instrumental in strengthening your brand. The first process in the business development stage is to have value. It is impossible for you to convincingly influence your future employer when you don't have a clear idea about your strengths or unique selling points. In other words, before others can believe in you, you need to believe in yourself! You need to be able to answer the question, "What value can you bring to this company?" To answer this question without quivering, you will need to have a firm grasp of what you have or that you know that can be valuable to another business. Take a few minutes to pause and reflect on the questions below:

1. What kind of value am I looking for from a future employer?
2. What assets, resources, and skills do I have that would be of value to a future employer?
3. What kind of growth opportunities should I be looking for that would help me become more valuable?

The second process in the business development stage is communicating your value. During this process, your efforts will be focused on convincing prospective employers of your value or getting them excited to work with you. Knowing how saturated industries have become with talent, you can imagine how challenging this task will be. To make your efforts more successful, you will need to ask yourself: Who will care about the value I offer? Consider the key individuals within organizations and the organizations as a whole. While it is unlikely to secure a job at Google on your first attempt, many organizations are looking for valuable employees like yourself. It would be of no use for you to approach those organizations who either aren't looking for what you have to offer or can't provide you with the value that you look for in an employer. Take another moment to pause and reflect upon the questions below:

1. Who will care about the value I have to offer them?
2. Who will be personally motivated to advocate on my behalf and help me through the organization's structure?
3. Who is the person or people that are positioned within the organization that holds the decision-making power to decide if I am worth pursuing?

The third process in the business development stage is delivering value. Arriving at this final stage of the business development journey means that you have successfully convinced others that you have the X-Factor. So far, you have not had to actively demonstrate the value that you promise to offer a future employer. However, at this point, you have probably secured an internship or temporary position at your desired company, and now it's time for you to deliver on your promises. Just as much as you put thought into the kind of value that you had to offer, you must continue to put the thought into your execution. Your value needs to come out through your interactions with customers, your work ethic, and relationships with your colleagues. In business, they always say, "every deal has a lifespan." This means that contracts that provide value now may become valueless in the future. Therefore, for your partnership with your employer to remain valuable, the partnership must continue to deliver value for both parties. Take a moment now, and reflect upon the questions below:

1. How can I ensure that my execution at work makes the partnership worthwhile?
2. How will I manage to deliver value as priorities and circumstances change?
3. How will my relationship with my employer and customers evolve over time?

EXERCISE: CREATE A VISION BOARD

Getting a job is not a smart goal—it's a binary outcome; you either have it or not. If you set that as a goal, you will be in a constant state of failure. YOUR GOALS NEEDS to be met daily. Instead of making your goal to secure a job, explore the many ways that you can improve upon the value you have to offer. By making yourself more attractive to future employers, you will be, in essence, marketing your value. Who can resist value when it is obvious for everyone to see?

As you refine your X-Factor, your sense of self-worth will increase. This is good news because the more you believe in yourself, the greater your ability to communicate your value. One of the ways that you can start expressing your value is by creating a vision board. A vision board is a collage of images and words, which communicate your aspirations and desires in life.

Vision boards are designed to be a source of inspiration to attain your goals. You are tasked to create a vision board relating to your life prospects, visions, and goals. You can design your board by taking a print out of all the pictures you want in your life—happiness, cars, house, family, etc.— and place that vision board near your bed. Every day when you wake up, your peripheral vision will see it and fill your subconscious mind with positive thoughts that will give you the energy to take action. These actions will give you positive results, and before you know it, you'll find yourself in a positive feedback loop whereby you are attracting more of the positivity you are sending out.

The positive feedback loop is like an ignition—you just have to get it started. When the going gets tough, you will remember your vision and where you want to end up in life. This will help motivate you and drive you to live a happy life with your family and not have to be in a constant state of worry about your financial situation.

2

YOUR MIND IS YOUR MONEY

U nemployment is a global issue affecting many households on both sides of the divide between rich and poor. More research is being carried out, measuring the impacts of unemployment on one's mental health. From as early as 1938, researchers were starting to see a correlation between poor mental health and unemployment. A review paper compiled by Eisenberg and Lazarsfeld in 1938 found that unemployment typically made people more emotionally unstable than they were before they were laid off (*Unemployment and Mental Health*, n.d.). Being unemployed is undoubtedly a stressful experience. Not only do you lose your job, but you also lose your steady source of income, personal work relationships, the daily routine and structure you had established in your life, and your sense of self-worth. The stress that an individual will experience during seasons of unemployment is measurable to the kind of stress one would experience if they were critically injured, going through a divorce, or mourning the passing of a loved one.

We cannot get away from it: the job market is a tough place for young people right now, and job hunting is often a stress-inducing, energy-sapping nightmare. Taking care of your mental health while you're job hunting becomes critical. Assessing how you are feeling and the quality of your thoughts should be a daily practice. Remember that this is only a period in your life and not a life sentence. Therefore, one of the best ways to spend your time during this period is to keep yourself preoccupied with career development, set goals for yourself, and create efficient job hunting processes, which will encourage you to use your mind and energy strategically.

STRATEGIES TO STAY RESILIENT DURING THE JOB HUNT

Finding a job when you're unemployed can be a daunting process. The pressure involved with the job hunt may be caused by personal circumstances which have forced you to get back on your feet as soon as possible. For instance, some stay-at-home mothers may have dedicated years in raising their children and taking care of the household; however, due to economic factors placing significant pressure on households, they are forced to get back into the corporate world. Being unemployed may make them feel guilty for not making a financial contribution to the operations of their household. This kind of situation is stressful and could lead to anxiety or, in severe cases, depression. Contributing to this hopeless feeling is the repetitive nature of the job search, which can be discouraging, especially after a few consecutive rejections.

These losses are hidden from the gaze of others because of how humiliating rejection can be. I have never seen a person update their LinkedIn status with, "I just received another rejection email from a job today; however, I believe a bot rejected me!" Most job seekers tend to conceal their feelings of frustration, which makes them sink deeper into their sense of hopelessness. Instead, the voice of their inner critic projects negative self-talk in their mind. They start to think, "Maybe I'm not as qualified as I think," "I'm unemployable," or "I need to settle for anything I can find." This negative self-talk attitude is not only unhealthy, but it can also sabotage job seekers' prospects of finding an ideal job. One solution to combat negative thinking and make the most out of the job-hunting process is to adopt an attitude of resilience.

Resilience is the ability to recover from difficult life events. It is a useful attitude to adopt as a job seeker because it will empower you to accept your present circumstance, adapt to its needs, and successfully move forward. Practicing resilience will help you bounce back from application rejection and commit to growing despite the unemployment woes. I would describe resilience as climbing up a mountain top without a trail map. Those who are not resilient would point out all of the disadvantages of climbing a mountain with no sense of clear instructions, while the resilient individuals would commit to creating a path as they walked. Even though resilient people still experience stress or fear, they refuse to allow the presence of fear to stop them from trying again and again until their breakthrough arrives. Eventually, after countless hours of walking, they reach the mountain top and smile as they look back at where they have come. Below are five strategies you can start practicing today that will improve your level of resilience during the job hunt:

1. Create Structure in Your Job Hunt

The job hunt is a tedious process that, at times, can be demotivating. Creating structure in your job hunting routine will encourage you to make the most out of hours spent searching. You can do this by creating a daily job hunting schedule that guides your job searching parameters. It will inform you of the number of hours you will spend each day on the job hunt and the other enriching activities you can incorporate in between to use your time constructively. Below is a sample of a typical daily job hunting schedule:

07:00 A.M: Wake up/prayer or meditation/breakfast outside

08:00 A.M: Start job hunting and filling in job applications

10:30 A..M: Go for a walk/listen to a podcast/write in your journal

12:00 P.M: Continue job searching and completing job applications

14:30 P.M: Make a healthy lunch/call a close friend or relative/run errands

16:30 P.M: Go to the gym/workout at home/take a swim

18:30 P.M: Prepare dinner/listen to a personal development audiobook

20:00 P.M: Enhance your skills/continue an online course/listen to videos of mentors or industry experts/learn a new skill

21:00 P.M: Read your affirmations/prayer or meditation/go to sleep

2. Work Smarter, Not Harder

Be strategic about your job hunting. When you desperately need a paycheck coming in, it can be tempting to apply for anything and everything. But this approach not only saps your energy, but it also doesn't work! Employers can tell when you're desperately applying for dozens of jobs that are irrelevant to your experience—and they don't like it. Instead, have a strategy in place. Know how many hours you want to work in your future workplace, in which area or department, and what you want your salary range to be—and whether you're willing to take something less exciting to you for the sake of experience and an income. When your time spent searching for a job is used efficiently, you won't need to put in many hours a day. It is also useful to identify the best career portals and websites that give you quality leads. Spend your time on these websites and set up alerts that notify you of new posts related to your industry or position of choice. Keep track of every job you apply for by setting up an excel spreadsheet. There is nothing worse than receiving a call from a recruiter after having forgotten that you applied to work at their company.

3. Confidence Is Contagious

Consistently receiving rejection emails can genuinely take a knock at your confidence. However, you should be comforted by the fact that rejection is normal, and it happens to everyone at least once during their job search. Your confidence is a tool that will help you remain resilient through the many lows that you will experience while job hunting. If your job search isn't making you feel any more confident than you already are, you should find other activities or interests that increase or maintain your confidence. Maybe you can volunteer at a local charity or take a position at a job that doesn't pay. These kinds of initiatives will make you feel like you are making a meaningful contribution in some way, thus boosting your confidence. Other methods of boosting your confidence are to practice self-care, explore some of your hobbies, or become a mentor to a young person. In essence, try to do anything that will make you feel like a winner, contributor, or hero, even if it is a small victory.

4. Build a Support System

When you are unemployed, the easiest thing to do is to self-isolate. I understand that the last thing you want to do while looking for a job is to socialize with other people. Not only does this activity seem expensive for your tight budget, but you may feel self-conscious about connecting with others who may be in better social standing than you. However, connecting with others during periods of stress is the most encouraging activity that you can do. It will help you feel like you are not alone and that your situation is relatable. At some point, your friends were also in the same position as you are, and so there is a lot of support that they can provide you. Talking with friends also allows you to network with people that may be in the industry that you desire to enter (they may be able to give you leads or valuable advice). A close friend may also be good for a simple venting session! Who better to listen to your frustrations than someone who knows your life journey? Going out for coffee with a friend and commiserating about your job hunting can be surprisingly cathartic.

WHY YOU NEED A CAREER DEVELOPMENT PLAN

Some people wait for their career to happen to them instead of being proactive and planning their career development. The executives at the top didn't get there by a miraculous occurrence; rather, it took time, effort, and, most importantly, planning. A career development plan is a useful document for both job seekers and those who are already employed. It includes a written summary of your career aspirations, objectives, areas of improvement, and your goals. Some of the key considerations that you will have to make when designing your career development plan include:

- Where are you in your career currently, and where do you want to be?
- What are some of your interests, dislikes, passions, strengths, weaknesses, skills, and experience? How

closely are these factors aligned with the kind of job you seek to pursue?

- What are your short-term and long-term career goals?
- What are some of the skills, qualifications, or experience that you still need to work on?
- What are some of the other job requirements and industry trends that you still need to research?

Your dream job is attainable once you have a clear vision statement written down. Moreover, setting clear and action-able goals will allow you to map the steps you need to take to navigate you toward your vision. Many people are tempted to formulate ideas in their minds and keep them in abstract form. I find that writing your vision and goals on paper gives you tangible evidence to refer back to when you are feeling overwhelmed. The document also makes you more accountable for achieving your vision because your progress is measurable. When designing a career development plan, flexibility is key. Make accommodations for the sudden and unexpected turns that life brings and adjust your vision and goals accordingly.

Find ways to remind yourself about the larger goals you have set daily, weekly, or monthly. You can do this by posting encouraging notes around your room or on your fridge or setting daily or weekly alerts on your phone. This process should be empowering and cause you to stay motivated to take baby steps forward. Therefore, prioritize one goal at a time and focus your energy on seeing it through. You can also record the baby steps you take in a career journal, detailing your thoughts, frustrations, and accomplishments on paper. This will help you keep track of all your career milestones and help you monitor your thought life.

The S.M.A.R.T Job Hunt

S.M.A.R.T goal setting is an effective tool to use for streamlining your job hunt. While this concept isn't new, it is still useful in helping you make the most out of your search. S.M.A.R.T is an acronym that stands for Specific, Measurable, Attainable, Relevant, and Time-bound (Johnson, 2019). Below is a breakdown of each of these elements and how they can help you find and secure your ideal job:

1. Specific

When you set vague goals, you will achieve vague results. Many job seekers believe that it is enough to search for any job with the keywords "job," "assistant," or "manager" in the title. This kind of strategy is like gambling and hoping to leave the casino with a million dollars that night. When you are more specific with your search, you save yourself time by only approaching organizations or applying for job posts related to the kind of work you intend to do. Therefore, you are encouraged to set clear goals for every aspect of your job search. You can do this by breaking your job search down into bite-sized components and setting a goal for each component. Some of the elements that you may consider includes:

- A list of targeted organizations
- Ways in which you can reflect and clearly identify your skills and abilities
- Your resume
- Your responses to commonly asked interview questions

2. Measurable

Your job-hunting goals should also be measurable. This will allow you to see whether your search is producing the quality of results you are hoping for. This will enable you to create benchmarks or indicators that notify you that you are on the right track. This is motivating, especially when you haven't secured a job yet. Instead of only celebrating once you have secured a job, measurable goals help you celebrate the smaller victories along the way. Quantifiable goals will also hold you accountable for the amount of effort you put in and make you feel as though you are making steady progress. Some of the considerations that you will need to make when setting measurable goals include:

- How many companies do you want to approach as part of your targeted list?
- How many applications do you want to submit per day or week?
- How many new connections do you want to make on LinkedIn per week?

3. Attainable

Your job-hunting goals are only useful when they are attainable. They must make sense according to your level of qualification and work experience. Applying for the position of a director when you have experience as a Team Manager is not realistic. It is also important to remember that aspects of your job search are out of your control. For instance, you cannot control how quickly a hiring manager responds to your application. Therefore, it is more empowering to set goals on the aspects of the job search you can control. This may include the number of hours you spend filling in applications or the attractiveness of your resume.

4. Relevant

The relevancy of your job hunting goals makes them more attainable and thus improves your favorable outcomes. It is easy to forget that the ultimate end goal is for you to secure a goal. Your job-hunting goals should always keep this overarching goal in mind. For instance, ask yourself how each goal is in some way helping you toward securing a job. Practicing this kind of initiative will help you keep your goals targeted. It will also reduce the amount of help you filter through job posts related to your career field and those that are not aligned with your desired outcome.

5. Time-bound

All of your job hunting goals should have a targeted time frame by which you should have completed them. It is important that your goals are not open-ended because this may cause you to be less proactive in securing a job. The aim is to give yourself a clear finish line for every goal you seek to achieve. You will be motivated to use your time wisely and focus only on the efforts which count. It will also give you a sense of accomplishment along your job seeking journey, making you feel productive in the pursuit of your ideal job.

EXERCISE: CREATING A LIFESTYLE OF GRATITUDE

It is important for you to remember to make time for your mental health and well-being throughout the job-seeking process. Just because you are in a vulnerable time in your life, it doesn't mean that you cannot find time for the things you enjoy. Spend time with your partner, friends, family, and pets. Keep up with your hobbies, get plenty of fresh air and some exercise, eat nourishing and healthy meals, get plenty of sleep, and allow yourself a treat every now and then. Develop a meditation or mindfulness practice. Write a journal entry every day. Ideally, you should be doing at least one thing that nourishes your physical or mental health and one thing that brings you joy every single day.

One life-producing exercise that you can practice during your free-times is showing gratitude. Gratitude is the assertion that you have everything that you will ever need now. It is the positive belief that there is something to be thankful for in each moment of the day. It doesn't take comparing your life with someone else's to practice gratitude; reflect on how far along in your journey you have come, and it will give you something to be thankful for. Make a list of all of the things you are grateful for each day. They can be big or small things. Read the list to yourself and feel the sensations of pure happiness, peace, or love that flows through you. This exercise will open your eyes to all the people and things you have in your life, and this realization will help you keep positive.

3

GETTING 'YOU' OUT THERE

As the job market has become more saturated with qualified people, it takes capitalizing on your unique attributes to get noticed by hiring managers. This is good news because it means your authenticity during the job search is a multiplier of your success. However, it also means that you need to focus on selling yourself instead of waiting to be discovered by your ideal place of work. When you think of selling yourself, you might think of a salesman trying to convince you to purchase a car. Looking for a job requires you to be the salesperson knocking on the right companies' doors and letting them know about the value that you have to offer. In essence, as a job seeker, you are trying to convince a company that your skills, experience, and knowledge are worth the investment.

When car sales associates desire to sell a car, they won't approach any random customer that walks through their showroom doors. In their minds, they understand their product so well that they know the kind of customer that will find that particular car valuable. For instance, the ideal buyer for a Lamborghini will never complain about the price because they can afford it. Similarly, you are precious cargo. It is important that you approach only those companies looking for candidates such as yourself and won't mind negotiating salary, contract terms, and employee benefits. Approaching companies that don't need what you are offering will lead to cold rejection and a bruise to your ego.

Furthermore, you need to understand the company or hiring managers you will contact. Every company is unique, even those that sell competing products and services. Each company has its own culture, structure, and vision, making it successful in the market. As much as you would love for your future employer to see your X-Factor, they would also appreciate it if you could see theirs. For instance, hiring managers can tell when a candidate's resume is a generic one distributed en masse to every company within the industry. A generic resume doesn't show the hiring manager enough evidence that you genuinely want to be a part of their team— if anything, it shows that you are desperate for any job. A desperate job seeker is seen as a liability to the company because their motives for applying may be out of self-interest. Therefore, you need to customize every piece of material you send to potential employers for their specific organization and show the recruiter that you appreciate the company's value.

HOW TO MARKET YOURSELF IN A JOB SEARCH

Your success in the job market rests on how well you understand yourself. When you genuinely believe in your unique value offer, you will find it easier to communicate with future employers. One way you can think about marketing yourself is to ask yourself if you were a brand, what would you stand for, and how would you want others to experience you? One of the secrets to successful job hunting is learning how to use some typical business-related marketing tools to promote yourself in front of relevant companies. Being a successful graduate, for example, is not only about securing a degree. It is more about developing important employability skills so that when you leave college, you have many examples to include in your job applications and interviews.

This means that as a young professional, it is vital to start building your professional brand while completing your studies. Those job seekers who have already completed their qualifications should use this short period of unemployment for career development and building a winning professional brand. To build your brand, ask yourself: what makes me stand out? It is pointless to highlight attributes that thousands of other accountants or graphic designers have in the competitive job market. Your brand is special only because you bring a distinct element to accountancy or an impressive graphic design.

Sometimes what makes you stand out is the extracurricular activities that you have engaged in related to your chosen profession. For instance, companies may appreciate the fact that you have taken on leadership roles in societal groups or unions in the past. Your active involvement in these groups is just another piece of evidence that boosts your employability. Volunteering at a local shelter or running your own charitable project will also show employers your level of commitment when it comes to a worthy cause. Volunteering within your community also sends a powerful message regarding your social consciousness. It communicates your ability to empathize with others and collaborate towards a greater initiative or project.

Optimize Your Online Persona

There's a job out there that you have been eyeing for a while. You meet all of the job specifications, and you have the confidence to back up your claims. Unfortunately, you are also aware that hundreds of job seekers meet the same requirements, so you are presented with a dilemma: how can

I get hiring managers to look at *me*? The simple modern-day solution is to create an online persona. Online personas are becoming so popular that many predict they will soon replace the resume. While a resume is a one page summary of your career history, online personas offer candidates unlimited space and fewer restrictions in selling themselves to potential employers.

Whether you are aware of it or not, you have an online brand. Your brand was slowly established by every piece of content you submitted online. If I were to access your social media accounts, what would your social media feed tell me about you? Would the content that I see reflect positively on you? While social media is a personal space, hiring managers can find source information about you through multiple online channels. A survey conducted by Reppler in 2011 showed that over 90% of hiring managers would visit a candidate's social media profile before considering whether to hire them or not (Fragiadaki, 2016). What was even more surprising was that 69% of these hiring managers confessed to passing on a candidate because of the negative social media presence they had found (Fragiadaki, 2016).

There's no doubt that recruiters rely more on information sourced online to make their hiring decisions. This doesn't mean that email communication is dead. However, it does emphasize the importance of managing your social identity and ensuring that it reflects the kind of woman or man that would fit into the culture of the industry of your choosing. For instance, a person in the creative arts has a lot of flexibility in the content they can post online because the creative industry embraces self-expression. However, a person in the private security industry cannot be as open online because they may compromise their clients' security or put themselves at risk. When hiring managers run a Google search on you, they are typically looking for three things. Firstly, they are looking to see if you have strong communication skills. Hiring managers will assess how well you communicate your ideas online and the quality of your interactions with others.

Secondly, they will look to see if you have a strong work ethic. Perhaps you have a blog, a few written articles, or post frequently on your social media accounts. These recruiters want to see the evidence of work that you have done in the past, which would prove that you are passionate about your job or a person who engages in social initiatives. Lastly, hiring managers are looking to see your sense of professionalism. As the saying goes, "it's not what you say; it's how you say it." Recruiters want to assess your behavioral conduct online and whether it would improve their organization's reputation or tear down their image. The encouraging news is that you have the power to control what you post online. If you are not who you used to be, then your online identity needs to be reorganized. All of the information about you online should emphasize your X-Factor and the qualities most suitable for the kind of career you seek to build for yourself. Below are four strategies for optimizing your online persona:

1. Do a Digital Clean Up

Most of our lives are documented online. During the job searching stage, you need to clean up your online identity. Immature statuses that you thought were cool when you were 13 years old may be considered offensive, degrading, or discriminatory in the liberal society we live in today. The first place to start the digital clean up is looking through all the photos and links that you are tagged in. Judging by the content, you may need to remove the tags or ask your friends to remove your name on the photo or link. Secondly, look back at your comments or comments on your photos from at least five years ago. Delete comments that are controversial or may not represent your current views and beliefs. You can also create a Google Alert to inform you every time your name is mentioned on social media, online articles, or blogs. This will help you manage your reputation online.

2. Participate in Professional Online Groups and Forums

Hiring managers are interested in finding out how much knowledge of the industry you have. Participating in industry or professional groups provides you with an opportunity to join relevant discussions and contribute your views on industry trends and updates. Your participation also shows recruiters that you are genuinely passionate about your work and would be an asset to their company. LinkedIn groups are a great place to start, offering you the platform to connect with other industry professionals and increase your professional reputation.

3. Ditch Microsoft Word, Embrace Online Graphic Design Tools

Back in the day, resumes were compiled as a Microsoft Word document that would, in some cases, stretch over four or five pages. Not only were these resumes unimaginative, but the formatting and layout of the document were not inspiring. With free online graphic design tools, it is easy to create a colorful branded resume, cover letter, email signature, and any other corporate branding that you need to establish your professional brand. Free graphic design websites like Canva provide job seekers with free tools to create resumes, infographics, slideshows, cover letters, and so much more. You can also use online tools to create a digital resume that is accessible through shareable links. The advantage of having a digital resume is that your resume is sourced easier when recruiters conduct relevant keyword searches online.

4. Create Your Own Website

Even though you may have an active social media presence, creating a website can make you stand out from the crowd! Your website would creatively showcase your career history, highlighting the work and projects you have done. It also allows hiring managers to get a feel for your personality and connect with you before the initial contact has been made. If you are not a programmer, you can use many website generating tools and sites to build your professional website with a click of a button. Otherwise, you can ask your technology-inclined friends or relatives to help you out. Include a 30 seconds elevator pitch on your website's homepage, which would captivate recruiters and sell you in the best light. Many online applications now have a section for you to include examples of your work or website; thus, you can include a link to your website in that section and add a link on your resume. As you progress in your career, keep the website updated, and remember to anonymize confidential information.

GET NOTICED!

It is challenging to feel as though you are not just a number or part of the many resumes heaped in a pile in an abandoned storeroom during the job search. The competitive nature of securing a job has made job seekers more creative in finding ways to stand out. Many job seekers see that their traditional method of finding employment—search for job posts, send a resume, and wait for a response—won't even get them through to the interview stage. New techniques for grabbing the hiring managers' attention have emerged, and some are highly ingenious.

Author Jim Krukal mentions the importance of ramping up your resume in terms of design and how you present it to your future employer. He speaks about a time in his own career where presenting a resume differently landed him a job immediately after graduating from college. He was passionate about working for that particular company, so he thought about ways to customize his resume for that particular job. One time during the interview stage, he happened to walk into the CEO's office and found the walls completely covered in post-it notes. When he asked the CEO to explain his office design, the CEO told Krukal that he liked to keep his ideas on notes because it keeps him organized and the ideas fresh in his mind.

Later that evening, Krukal thought that it would be a good idea to use the CEO's love for post-it notes as a way to make his resume stand out to him. The next day he purchased a large white poster board and several packets of yellow post-it notes. On each post-it note, he wrote a quality that he believed made him suitable for the job. He commissioned help from his fiancee, who had lovely handwriting, and together they came up with 50 qualities. He then arranged the notes on the poster board one-by-one, imitating the CEO's office walls. The next morning, Krukal dropped off his project with the CEO's secretary, along with another copy of his resume. About an hour later, Krukal received a call from the CEO, offering him the position he had applied for. On the call, the CEO told Krukal how he was the only candidate who went through so much effort to stand out.

EXERCISE: SEND A VIDEO MESSAGE

Want to really leave a memorable first impression? Why not send a video message to the hiring manager, letting them know why you are the best candidate for the job? Use the video to informally introduce yourself and explain how you can add value to their organization. Ensure that you include ways they can connect with you further and any valuable links to your online pages. Your video's quality is of utmost importance; a poorly shot video can negatively impact your professional brand. Therefore, practice getting the lighting, audio, and message sounding and looking professional. Upload the video on your website or a professional website like LinkedIn—LinkedIn algorithm favors media posts, and your reach will be far greater than a simple post composed of just text.

4

THE CIRCLE YOU NEVER KNEW EXISTED

The importance of networking when job hunting is still not understood and embraced by many job seekers. Perhaps it is because job seekers favor the traditional non-engaging method of finding employment. There are many excuses that they will come up with as justifications for not building a network. "My studies take up too much time," "I don't have rich friends," or "I don't have the money to attend fancy events." These common excuses also point to a misunderstanding of what true career networking entails. Career networking is not similar to a public relations campaign where you mingle with your city's socialites and attend fancy gala dinners. It also doesn't require as much time as many would assume. To simply put it, career networking is all about building relationships with just about anybody in the job market.

These could be relationships with your friends who work in the same industry, relationships with those who work in your desired company, or any industry gatekeeper. The myth about finding a job is that the most qualified candidate will secure the position. In most cases, companies are not lacking in skills or talent; thus, they are not as focused on qualifications or experience as much as we might think. The one thing that any company favors over qualifications is relationships. Let's face it—would you feel comfortable working so closely with someone you didn't know? You would need time to develop trust with that particular individual to open yourself up to them fully. Similarly, companies prefer to hire candidates they have already formed a relationship with because they are seen to be more trustworthy and familiar.

I guarantee you that if you spend more time building career relationships, you will never experience job insecurity ever again. This is because you will have so many career networks across multiple industries that will give you preferential treatment when you are looking to develop in your career. Networking is not a skill you learn for when you are desperate for a job. Rather, it is something that you practice and consistently work on so that your career relationships can deepen and become more fruitful. You need to have strong networks, whether you are in a stable full-time job or currently going in between jobs. So to answer the question of "When should I start building my network?" I suggest that you start NOW! Every day that you spend without meeting someone you know or engaging with industry professionals online is an opportunity gone to waste. Remember that the competition in the job market is not necessarily surrounding skills but more so related to who you know and the amount of access you have into a given company.

THE DARK SIDE OF THE JOB SEARCH

The common assumption about career networking is that it is an aggressive method of self-promotion. This cannot be further from the truth. The true purpose of networking is to form relationships with industry people, create a network of support, share advice, and expose each other to career opportunities. Indeed, networking is a two-way street. Regardless of your position, there is always someone below you who can benefit from your expertise and networks, and similarly, there is someone above you who can expose you to their network too. Thus, the more useful you are to others, the greater the assistance you will receive in your time of need. Being useful can range from simply mentoring or sharing career advice with a college student to submitting a friend or colleague's job application on their behalf to a hiring manager you know personally.

Building a network may very well be your ticket to a company. You're probably thinking, "If access to a company relies on networks, why do companies insist on posting or advertising job vacancies online?" This a great question, and to answer it, I would need to share the dark side of the job search with you. When applying for a job, everything is not always as it seems. Much of the job vacancies you see posted online are merely posted for transparency and not necessarily because a company is looking for a candidate online. Think of it this way, if you were a company and had over 1,000 submissions for a job vacancy, would you take the time to assess each submission? Probably not. As qualified as the 1,000 candidates may be, it would take too long to go through each cover letter and resume. Instead, you would first look internally in your organization for anyone that meets the job specifications because at least they are familiar with your organization's processes and culture, right? Assuming that you couldn't find anyone internally, you would ask for referrals from your trusted network of people who would then send you a more manageable number of applications that you could then look through.

Companies want to hire people who won't need too much training or upskilling because that costs time and money. Ideally, a company looks to hire a candidate who is familiar with how things operate within the organization and can get to work immediately. The sad reality is that only 7% of job seekers land a job from an employee referral, even though referrals account for around 40% of all job hires (Saven, 2015). This means that having someone within an organization put in a good word for you could help your job application considerably and give you an advantage in the competition. Another dark truth about the job search is that 80% of all jobs are never posted online; rather, they are advertised through networks. I know how frustrating this can be, especially when you have worked so hard to make yourself employable and have a stellar professional brand. However, look at it this way: the skills you have built and the brand you have forged are only useful when the right people know about them. Therefore, you cannot discount the importance of communicating your capabilities through a network of powerful people.

Spending hours on the Internet filling out job applications is just not enough. Indeed, online job vacancies give you an indication of what is out there in the job market, but for the 80% of jobs that are not advertised (most of the time, these include the kind of job you are looking for), you will need to connect with people to access them. Hence it is just as important to make time for face-to-face meetings, catch-up sessions, and industry-related socializing as you carry out your job hunt and after you have secured a job. You can take baby steps to build your network by first mapping out the people that you know. You can do this by creating a list of former colleagues, classmates, project members, and so forth.

After, set up a coffee date with the people on this list and learn more about their role at work, their experiences in the corporate world, and any advice or suggestions they have for you in your job hunt. When requesting to meet up with them, your text message can go along these lines: "Hi Steven. I'm really interested in exploring the many ways I can grow in my career, and I noticed on your LinkedIn profile that you are doing very well for yourself. I would love to take you out for coffee and learn more about your experiences in the corporate environment. Will you be available to meet up soon?"

SOCIAL NETWORKING ON SOCIAL MEDIA

To gain knowledge or access the hidden jobs that are not advertised online, look for recruiters, contacts, and anyone you know in a company that you want to work for and ask them about job openings. Don't be shy to contact a recruiter on LinkedIn and introduce yourself to them and let them know your area of expertise. After, make it a point to comment on their posts and regularly engage with them so that you remain fresh in their mind when they are looking to fill new vacancies. Secondly, maximize the power of word of mouth. The process works like this: a person you know knows someone who is hiring and then refers you to them. What you may not know is that most of these types of referrals are from second-level connections (people who are connected to your friends, relatives, or colleagues). Networks are powered by word of mouth because you have to be brave enough to ask your circle of friends whether there is a job opening that they know about. More importantly, hiring managers need to have their ears on the ground, listening for leads to talented candidates.

Therefore, the benefit of having a network is that you get information about employers that are open to hiring new people and employers and, in turn, hear about suitable candidates. Professional networking starts with identifying one's competencies and learning to speak about them to that potential network. Once again, it is crucial that you learn how to communicate your X-Factor to the relevant people appropriately. One of the best communications strategies nowadays is to follow professionals on LinkedIn and regularly post status updates or share interesting links. Through your LinkedIn network and your own personal connections, you'll find out about industry events you can attend and start meeting people in person.

Remember to also think about what it is that you can give to others. Reflect on the skills, knowledge, and expertise you have that could be useful to your contacts. Think about how you can be helpful. The key ingredients of social networking are trust and reciprocity. For instance, you can create a tweet on Twitter, linking companies to your website, your portfolio, or digital content that you think they will find awesome. Your tweet could even say something like, "Hey @Google, I applied to your open marketing position. Here's a link to my short elevator clip in case you missed it!" While this move is public and quite bold, it will help you get back on their radar after a job application and demonstrate your willingness to stand out from the crowd.

There are many other ways that you can use Twitter to your advantage. For instance, you can ask your network on Twitter to share opportunities with you. Find threads or trending industry hashtags to post your work or job hunt status on–your network might be able to connect you to some cool opportunities! The truth is that people feel good after helping someone else meet a need. Therefore, your job hunt status is not a burden to your network, and you should never feel embarrassed to ask for help or a leg up publicly. Even requesting your network to simply "Retweet" your status will increase the level of reach that it has on the platform, allowing you to be visible to a greater pool of people.

Social networking can also take place offline and in real-time! There are always some professional events happening within close proximity to your school or home where industry experts are speaking on any given weekend. You can browse through websites of town halls, convention centers, and local universities or colleges to find out more about upcoming industry events, guest lectures, or talks. Sometimes these events may take place on weekdays; however, most of them are free to attend. If you have some time to spare in between your daily routine, attending one of these industry events would be an excellent opportunity to generate more leads. You can also check to see which speakers are hosting the event or talk and view their online profile before attending the event. This will give you insight on how to approach them and the relevant questions to ask.

Your objective is to make yourself stand out during these industry events by engaging with the speakers and making them interested in you. Your strategy to achieve this is simple—before you go to an event, research the topic the speaker will speak about and prepare one question to ask publicly in an open Q&A session. Afterward, when you socialize, you will approach them and thank them for their time in answering the question. This will help you create a warmer and more familiar relationship with the speaker. CLEARLY MENTION your interest in them or in what they do. For example, you might say something like, "I would love to work for a leader like you and a similar cause." It is important not to ask for a job or an interview while getting to know them. The following step is to immediately jump to your ethical bribe, something of value for the other person. This will create the reciprocity that all successful networking requires. For example, you can offer to share your research paper or book with them. Gently TELL the speaker that you would be happy to send a copy of it via email.

NOW YOU have suddenly added value to their career. Once they respond, create a cover letter of no more than 500 words highlighting your relevant experience and greatest achievements. You should use real figures when explaining your contributions in previous companies. For example, instead of saying, "I have saved company X £10,000" and risk sounding disingenuous, it would be better for you to say, "I have saved company X £10,356." Once the speaker has received your free gift and a copy of your cover letter, they will either give you an interview, connect you to associates that may be looking for somebody like you in their organization, or have you in their mind. All of these possible outcomes are great because they will get you a step closer to meeting the right people with the right job offer.

THE EMAIL THAT SECURED A JOB!

Networking has become an indispensable component of building a successful career. More job seekers realize that securing a job is more about being likable than anything else. The ability to find, cultivate, and capitalize on professional relationships become your competitive edge during the job hunt. Natalie Fredrette's networking success story shows how powerful sending a few emails to the right person can be after graduating from college (Fredrette, 2019):

"With my LinkedIn profile and resume polished, I began getting lots of contacts from recruiters that resulted in follow-up phone meetings with hiring managers. This gave me great experience in asking critical questions about company goals, daily work styles or objectives, and company fit. Out of 5 phone screens, I got 3 follow up phone interviews and 1 on-site invitation that did not result in an offer. All the while, I kept working hard in my lab and networking. And here comes the sudden crazy twist: three and a half years ago, when I was a newly-minted Ph.D. graduate in vascular biology, my dad (being a classic dad) had been "bragging" about his daughter at a completely unrelated event.
One of his colleague's spouses mentioned that she'd be happy to hear more about my work. So, dad told me to email her when I had my conference in San Francisco (her home city). We met for breakfast. I didn't know her quite well, so I just thought it would be a nice morning talking to another scientist. It turns out she was a team director of a medium-sized

R&D company in the bay area. THANK GOOD-
NESS I had no idea before I met her!!!! I probably
would have clammed up. I sent her my long-winded
CV after breakfast. Over the next few years, I would
contact her every six months or so just to say
congrats on her work in a pharma trial or tell her
about a paper I thought was interesting.
These emails were usually bare-bones dialogue,
overall just providing value in small ways over these
3.5 years. Finally, my transition began with a short,
simple email that went like this:
'Hi XX, congrats on the new data! I see your FDA
trial had a really impressive outcome for XXX, and I
know that your extra data points will assuage any
concerns about XXX criticism. Looks like XXX
biology saves the day again. ☺'
I got an email 2 minutes later. One of the ideas we
had talked about years ago was actually something
her company decided to pursue, and they had
become extremely busy! She asked if I was looking
around for new opportunities. She wanted me to
send her a resume and fly out to California as soon as
possible. I asked about a cover letter she said, no
need for that; just put me as your reference, and
they'll know you're good to go. The simple act of
emailing someone a couple of times a year got me an

interview that eventually led to an incredible job offer."

Natalie's networking success story proves that the focus on all of our networking efforts should be placed on building strong relationships over time. Of course, if you happen to meet a company director at a networking event and manage to speak to him or her for 10 minutes, they would have forgotten your name by the time they leave the event. However, if you take time to carefully nurture the relationship with the director (without being too forward or pushy), the bond between you will be much deeper. It took Natalie years for her relationship with the director to pay off; nonetheless, when it did, the rewards were more than what Natalie could have asked for! Therefore, I urge you to think of professional networking as a long-term investment.

You will be required to invest your time and energy into relationships that may only reward you in the years to come. However, once trust has been earned through numerous engagements and communication, your professional relationships will protect and provide for you as long as the relationship stands. Below are three golden rules for successful networking that will cause you to build fruitful professional relationships.

Golden Rule 1: Be a Giver

Everyone loves to be associated with a generous person. This is largely because it is assumed that generous people have a lot of value to offer. Consider a director who dedicates a portion of his or her earnings every year for charitable giving. The assumption from their display of generosity would be that the company is paying him or her very well, or they have other private investments that generate a lot of revenue. Regardless of the validity of these assumptions, professionals from all levels will want to network with this director because of the potential value that they may offer one day. If you are unable to give money, look in your career toolkit and see what else you can give. What about your long list of skills or talents? These can be used as your currency in networking and offered freely when the opportunity arises.

Golden Rule 2: Be a Joiner

Successful networking also involves being a part of organization groups or societies. However, you are expected to do a lot more than merely sign on to become a member and attend every monthly meeting. Remember golden rule number one? It applies here too! Use your membership in groups to offer your skills or talents for free. You can do this by finding an activity or priority within the group that interests you. You can also start working toward joining the group's committee, mini-project groups, or administration board, so your value within the organization is publicly seen. The beauty of joining these professional groups is that you can make friends who may work at companies you could only dream of working in. As your contribution and status in the group continue to grow, your professional reputation will also increase. Eventually, your reputation will travel, and many opportunities for career growth will follow.

Golden Rule 3: Be a Caretaker

All of the relationships you make while generously giving your time or participating in groups must be nurtured. Every relationship that is made during the course of your career development counts—including the relationship you have with the office cleaner, tea lady, and receptionist. One of the ways that you can show that you care is by being consistent. Remember the small things like people's names or brief information about their lives and make sure that your conversation is meaningful (even when it is short). If you were available to assist people with their work tasks at the beginning of your career, you would need to make time to attend to their requests even after a few promotions. Your reputation is built over numerous encounters that people have with you, and therefore, it is important to stay consistent in how you choose to show up for people and add value to their lives.

EXERCISE: CREATE A COMPANY BUCKET LIST

Build a company bucket list of 5 to 10 companies you want to work for and then connect with five people from each company. Obviously, a referral by a shared connection is your best bet. However, if you don't have a shared connection, you will have to step out of your comfort zone and try to connect with strangers. This is not as hard as you think. You can customize a request to connect on LinkedIn or even use an Inmail to write a longer email asking to connect. Your goal here is to ask them to connect in hopes of you learning more about the company and what it might take to earn a position there. Stress that you aren't looking for them to help you get a job; rather, all you desire is an insight into what the process is like in their work environment. Not everyone will accept your invitation to connect with them, but this is a numbers game. Out of the five people in each company, you only need at least one person to connect with and speak to, and you can use that connection to build many others in the future!

5

THE HIDDEN SECRETS OF A HIGH PAYING CAREER

The advice that many are given when seeking jobs is to accentuate their positive attributes; however, after securing a job and having to give their performance review or accept daily feedback, the emphasis is always on what can be done better. Our interactions with colleagues, managers, and sometimes even coaches can make us experts at accommodating others' strengths without capitalizing on our own. Of course, this works against us in the long run because, according to findings from Gallup, employees who use their strength every day at work are six times more likely to perform better at their job and improve the company's overall profitability (Dishman, 2015). What's frightening is that most positions are filled with qualified yet unproductive people who aren't maximizing all of their strength.

Take a moment to pause and reflect on your professional strengths. Are you even aware of them? Tasks or job positions that energize you are not necessarily your strengths. For instance, you might be great at sales-related jobs; however, after closing every deal, you envision yourself never having to answer another sales-related call again. It is important to find your professional strengths because this information will direct you toward an ideal career path. Not only that, your strengths will help you position yourself in an organization and leverage your gifts to progress at work. The common mistake that people make is to base their career decisions on how much money the job offers or the status associated with the job. Sooner or later, they are dissatisfied with their job, and as a result of their negative perceptions, they cannot identify opportunities to progress in the company.

STRENGTH = CAREER LONGEVITY

This chapter will be controversial to some and refreshing for others—I will make you challenge your past decisions to set you on the right career path. Some of what I have to share with you might feel uncomfortable, but that's okay. You're not reading this book because you're seeking validation; you're reading this because you want to regain complete control over your career prospects. Here's a truth to start you off: even if you are a skilled and talented professional, if you are not in the right field, you will lose due to reasons beyond your control. Working in the wrong field is like purchasing a luxurious house in a crime-ridden neighborhood. The tenant you find wants to leave every year or two, and you're always looking for new tenants. As beautiful as the house is, its location brings the property's value and its desirability down. Similarly, when you have exceptional skills and talent but are in the wrong field, your value quickly diminishes.

When many job seekers choose their careers, they are significantly influenced by the job's salary. I agree that salary is an essential criterion in selecting the ideal job; however, there are other factors more important than a paycheck at the beginning of your career. It is important to note that ideal career fields reward you the most as you mature in the industry and gain more experience. While you may need to put in extra hours in the beginning and hop from one job title to the next, you will enjoy the benefits that career longevity has to offer after a while. Your years of experience will pay off, and you won't ever have to worry about job insecurity because you would have years of networking and experience under your belt!

Some people may have difficulty accepting this because we live in a "get rich quick" world that has come to resent long-term gratification. Nonetheless, just like any stock market investment, the best returns are earned over many years. The only legitimate career that could offer you wealth within a short amount of time is entrepreneurship; however, the amount of time, money, and networking you must invest in your business is more than the average worker. Therefore, as much as you can try to find loopholes in the career development process, you cannot escape the time it takes to build and sustain a career. Choose to look at your career as being a 4-decade journey. The amount of money you make at the beginning of your career doesn't have much bearing in the long run. As you learn, grow, and network, your salary will increase accordingly.

Using the stock market investing analogy once again, you want your investment (or career in this case) to grow steadily, giving you more money every year and enjoying higher yields as time goes by. This will grant you the ability to increase your standard of living by achieving that six-figure salary that you desire so much. In the long run, you will have enough money to purchase your dream family home, splurge on summer vacations, and take on expensive hobbies—as long as you stay on the right track and become intentional about your career development. Regardless of how old you are, it is never too late to take a grip on your career and turn it around!

The second essential criteria for choosing an ideal career field is job security. Our jobs are an essential part of our survival because they are our primary source of income. When we have job security, we can plan our lives comfortably and create a lifestyle within our means. Alternatively, when prospects of work are not stable, we cannot sustain a decent career or enjoy the peace of mind that comes with knowing that our job will always be in demand. As your value increases in the job market—due to your experience— you will also want to become high in demand, so you don't have to worry about unemployment again. Even after enduring one unemployment patch, you can experience devastating losses with your career, wealth, and happiness. Recovering from one of these career low points may mean that you have to take a lower role to pay some of your recurring bills. Although necessary for survival, this desperate move may take you off your career trajectory to the extent that you are unable to recover.

It is also worth noting that certain fields always face job insecurity regardless of your experience. This is due to a wide range of factors, including economic pressures, technological advancements, and globalization. Most of the career fields affected by job insecurity tend to be lower-skilled occupations such as telemarketing, welding, waitressing, or construction work. Career fields that were highly specialized and demanded a greater skill level tend to offer greater job security. Most of these highly-skilled occupations include dentistry, law, analysts, and doctors. Another threat to job security is unemployment— a lot of companies consider you unemployable if you have been unemployed for longer than six months. Yes, this isn't fair, but that's the way the job market goes. It can be discouraging to hear that you are unemployable only because it has taken you a little longer to find work after graduating or going out of the job market briefly to raise your children. This kind of rejection opens you up to a life of constant misery and fear, which you want to avoid at all costs.

One way you can use the employment gaps productively is by seeing them as your "business development" phase—as alluded to in chapter one—where you find ways of upskilling yourself. For instance, you can complete a course, sign up for a training program, or look into new ventures. You can write a brief note on your cover letter informing the hiring manager that you were upskilling yourself and adding more value to your professional brand during your periods of unemployment. This will demonstrate exceptional time management skills as well as display your resilience. As a result of your proactiveness, your temporary period of unemployment would not be a loss in any way.

PRACTICAL EXAMPLES FOR CHOOSING THE IDEAL CAREER

Let's get practical now so you can apply this knowledge to your own career field and find out if you are wasting your time in your job or actually building a strong career. Even if you discover that you are wasting your time, you have nothing to worry about because I'm going to share with you actionable suggestions to turn your prospects around for good!

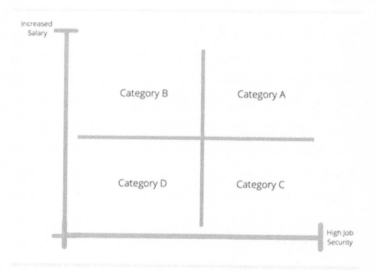

Case study: You are a Retail Banker

Pretend that you are a retail banker. You get to enjoy an increased salary every year and eventually become a bank manager earning $100,000+ in your mid to late 30s. Great life, right? It fits the first criterion (increased salary), but it doesn't fit the second criterion—it doesn't have high job security. There's a limit of branches to manage, and it's a very specific role to that particular bank with its own unique internal systems and services. Because of this, you are under constant threat from upcoming managers. It also means that if your branch closes down, you move houses or get bored with your job, you won't sustain your living standards anymore. Although it pays really well, your job dictates where you live and other lifestyle decisions. All those years spent studying and networking to become a branch manager have led you to build a valuable yet vulnerable career for yourself.

If you changed your occupation and you were now a Certified Public Accountant (CPA), you would fit in the category of high job security, but it wouldn't reward you much in the long term. While you may never see an unemployment period in your career, the salary ceiling will always remain. The appropriate question to ask at this point is: what kind of jobs provide you with job security or insecurity? How do top performers manage to retain their jobs for so many years? The benefit of highly-skilled or highly-demanding occupations is that they come with high-entry barriers. These barriers keep a supply of candidates in check while also reducing the level of competition once inside the field.

Conversely, job insecurity comes when there are low-entry barriers. The lower the entry barriers are, the greater the competition and thus, the lower the demand for the occupation becomes. Please note, by "entry," we are not referring to entry-level jobs that a graduate would seek; rather, we are talking about entering at any level of seniority and experience.

To understand the barriers to entry, we can use an analogy of building a wall. Generally speaking, the more bricks you lay on a wall, the more difficult it is for trespassers to come in and threaten your position. In other words, when there is a low demand for your job (due to the high-entry barrier), the fewer reasons your employer will have to let you go—high barriers keep the supply and demand dynamics in check (i.e., limited supply). This is really important in times of economic recession when the first people to be considered redundant are those in occupations with low-entry barriers. Therefore, to have peace of mind at work, you must ensure that you build a high wall for yourself and make your role indispensable. For example, the first brick on your wall may be a bachelor's degree. Now ask yourself this question: can people do your job without a degree? For example, if you are an accountant or lawyer, it is a prerequisite that you have a degree before you are selected for the role. Going one step further, would a master's degree be a requirement for your job? Or how about a Ph.D.? (AI researchers are Ph.D. qualified).

Without a CPA, you can't work as a public accountant, and even nowadays, in project management, it is difficult to enter the field without PRINCE2 qualification. Having the Qualifying allows you to speak the same language as the rest of the team. Moreover, a marketing professional cannot apply for an accountant's role because the two career paths have very different entry criteria. So by assessing the requirements needed to qualify for a particular career field, you eliminate people without a degree, those without special training or certifications, as well as those who have not written specific exams. Translate this to your own field and evaluate your own position. However, as a CPA qualified accountant, despite your job being secure, the role doesn't get more complex the more years you're in the field, so you won't necessarily enjoy a significantly increased salary. In other words, you will reach the ceiling of expertise quickly because your employer won't be able to justify an increase in salary.

The biggest—and probably the most influential—brick on the wall is the progression of your profession's complexity. If you are in a career field where your role's complexity gets more advanced with more years on the job, your job becomes more secure. This will also be a huge contributor to the first criteria, which is an increased salary. This is good news because it means that you get to enjoy job security and an increased salary as your job becomes more complex. Can you imagine the complexity involved in managing huge million dollar projects? Consider the project manager who was in charge of building the Burj Khalifa in Dubai. Can you imagine how many decades of experience the project manager had to have before they could consider him or her for the job? Their income and job security are in proportion to the complexity of the problems they have had to solve throughout their career. This kind of career opportunity wouldn't be accessible to a person who had graduated from college just three years ago. However, it does reassure the young architecture graduate that the nature of his or her field can reach incredible heights in terms of its complexity, and thus it is a great career field to explore.

TARGETING HIGH PAYING, HIGH-SECURITY JOBS

When targeting high-paying, high-security jobs, it is crucial for you to first learn which jobs NOT to aim for. This doesn't mean that these low paying or low-security jobs are not fulfilling. There may be some of you who have studied to enter these particular career fields and are highly motivated to work in them. This is great! However, the only downfall that you will find with these low paying or low-security jobs is that salary and career growth are usually capped at a certain threshold. Once you have reached the highest possible salary benchmark, it is nearly impossible to earn any higher or upskill yourself any further. An example of a career with low job security and salary potential—and please forgive me if you are in this field, but I need to be honest for your sake—is the Human Resources department, also known as HR.

As mentioned above, your career is a four-decade journey, which ideally is meant to steadily develop as you learn more skills and gain more work experience. Unfortunately, HR is not a technical field, and so there is little to learn. In other words, you don't need to be highly skilled to perform HR duties. Once you have learned all there is to know about Human Resources, you won't be required to learn anything else—from then onward, you follow the specific processes and protocols to effectively perform your job. Unlike other career fields, you don't become a better HR professional after years of experience. Indeed, you may be wiser, which would justify a slight increase in value and pay; however, it was a promotion based on age and not on becoming more qualified for the job.

A junior hire with two years of HR experience and someone with 20 years of experience won't have much difference in pay. What is even more disheartening is that a fresh graduate can easily replace a 40-year old HR professional. The graduate may see this and become ecstatic, thinking that their new skills or magnetic personality led the company to replace someone with decades of experience. However, what the graduate doesn't know is that this same process will also happen to them in the future when another innocent graduate comes to take their position. Other job seekers may believe that category B jobs are the best option in the quadrant. Category B jobs are those that offer higher salaries but lower job security. The unfiltered truth is that all category B jobs are not passion-driven; instead, they are supposed to be money-driven or financial security-driven careers.

A job seeker would decide to go into these kinds of career fields to live a comfortable and luxurious life—in the shortest possible time frame. They are less concerned about longevity and more concerned about earning as much money as they can now. The ironic thing about these professionals is that they desire to be honored with the same recognition as one would give a professional who has earned their way up the corporate ladder through time and dedication to their craft. I cannot say it any other way: if you want to be an Olympian of the corporate world, you've got to pick an Olympic sport! Your stone-throwing skills may earn you a lot of money in a short period of time; however, they won't qualify you for the Olympic games!

Lastly, high-paying and high-security jobs require exceptional skill levels. This has nothing to do with your employer; it's more about the skills you acquire along your career development journey. You may have a multinational employer listed in your resume but may still be in category D (low job security and low salary) on your quadrant due to your job. Take a moment and think about your transferable skills. Transferable skills are the expertise that you can use in many job roles or occupations. Some job seekers ignorantly chase after the status that comes with working at a recognizable company and settle on a low skilled position within that company. How do you think this would reflect on their next job search? Do you think their next employer will be so impressed by the fact that they worked at a reputable company and neglect their low skilled role? Of course not.

It is always better to aim for as much responsibility as you can get in any company you work for. This will allow you to gain a considerable amount of experience in each role. It also means that you can breathe a sigh of relief if you prefer to work for smaller companies or agencies. The size of the company won't count for much when you are listing your work experience anyway. It is vital that you don't sell your career and future short for a low skilled role for the sake of a brand name. Once more, if your job falls in category D, you're taking almost the same amount of risk as an entrepreneur, not knowing if the cash flow will be enough for tomorrow or whether the company will survive a few economic downturns or political instability. The only difference between you and the entrepreneur is that your job comes without any promise of potential benefits.

On the other hand, entrepreneurs can justify taking that risk because the upside exists—the benefits can be tremendous if the company survives. If your big brand employer survives another year, you could continue in your job, however, maintaining a mediocre salary. It simply isn't worth it.

How Do I Get Myself to Category A?

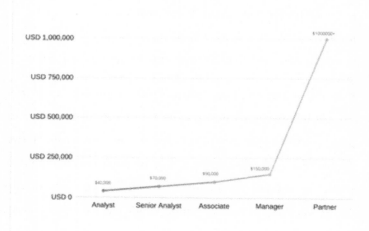

Let's look at management consulting jobs as an example. The line graph above shows us that the pay in this career field rises gradually throughout the stages from associate consultant to director and partner level. When you become a partner, you enter the category A+ territory and can potentially make millions per year. Those with a discerning eye would have noticed how the salary pay, as shown on the graph, jumps from $200,000+ on a manager/director level to a seven-figure million-dollar income at partner level. So what changed between the two roles? It's simple: the partner is no longer handling B2B client relationships. Instead, they are in charge of bringing in revenue and contributing directly to the bottom line (profit/loss) growth. That makes all the difference!

I understand that this may sound alien to you because you've never been exposed to this part of corporate life before—not a lot of people have. Nevertheless, if you are strategic about how you plan your career development, a dynamic and successful career is within your grasp; it is possible! Even if your field doesn't allow you to reach an A+ level, that's absolutely fine. Category A jobs still offer plenty of money, and you will have more free time with less category A+ responsibility. You can gradually put money away and make financial investments with your surplus cash.

You can still aim for that category A job that will provide you with your desired lifestyle and the ability to invest. This means that you don't have to be a business owner to enjoy a luxurious lifestyle; category A jobs will give you that life of stability without the fear of being unemployed. The category A kind of life is a life with the most gifted and smartest professionals who help you improve and, more importantly, help you create the life you want. However, this kind of career success begins with your brutal and honest self-evaluation!

6

DECODING THE COMPETENCY
NOISE

W hen employers consider which candidates to hire for job vacancies, they will look at several factors. For instance, they will consider the candidate's level of experience, their knowledge about the role, the amount of training they have received in the past, and the skills required for the position. After ticking all of these boxes, employers will then implement a thorough competency-based recruitment process to ensure that they are not only good on paper. Competency-based recruitment is becoming a new way of securing new talent into a company. It involves hiring candidates for their qualifications and their proven track record of offering exceptional value to their previous employers.

It's not enough for candidates to be book smart. Nowadays, companies want to know how you will deal with stress, customers, and unexpected challenges from real experiences you have come across. Knowing this information would put the employer at ease because it would show them that you won't panic under pressure or cause problems at work. Competency-based recruitment approaches use several assessments that are designed to help hiring managers identify those candidates who have valuable skills and response mechanisms that will support them in their daily tasks at work. It also allows the hiring manager to get to know the candidate personally and understand their personality better before progressing to the next phase of the hiring process.

Candidates also benefit from competency-based recruitment because it allows them to demonstrate their X-Factor by giving examples of how they were effective in previous job roles. This is good news, especially for candidates whose resume or cover letter was not as polished as it could have been. In essence, it is an opportunity to meet your future employer in person and sell what you have written on your resume. Throughout this process, you can strategically market yourself to communicate the kind of message you want the hiring manager to receive. For instance, you would refer to previous incidences where you demonstrated excellent teamwork, time management, or problem-solving skills. This would show the hiring manager that you will be an asset to their company, beyond the skills that offer.

12 TOP COMMON COMPETENCIES HIRING MANAGERS LOOK FOR

Candidates who can demonstrate having the right attitude and behavior are seen as being the most competent. Competency has been used as a judge of character and job fit because a candidate's employability and suitability for the role can be seen through their attitude. For instance, an IT customer service representative may be highly skilled at performing their job and fixing computers. However, if they cannot arrive on time for their interview with the hiring manager, it would prove that they are incompetent in time management. Assessing competency also helps hiring managers determine the level at which candidates can perform. For instance, a hiring manager may ask you to tell them where you see yourself in five years because they want to assess how much progress you see yourself making in the company.

No one is born being competent at performing their job duties. Becoming skilled at what you do requires time and effort spent practicing and studying how to effectively perform professional tasks and work with others. You don't need to have a job before you can start building your competence for your desired position or career field. All you need to do is fill up your day with activities that require you to have some level of responsibility, focus, or skill to perform effectively. For example, as a job seeker, you can practice communicating effectively with others by networking or learning how to work well in a team by volunteering at a local charity. You need to keep in mind that each career field may demand different competencies. Therefore, make a list of all the competencies related to your career field and start practicing them today!

When deciding on which competencies are the most appropriate for you to learn in your chosen career field, you will need to make the following considerations:

- What will be my level of decision-making or authority in my job position?
- How much internal collaboration and interaction will be required?
- How much contact and interaction with customers will I be required to do?
- What level of physical skills and knowledge will I need for the job?

For grass root employees, the level of physical skills and knowledge forms a large portion of the competencies required for the job. This is due to the lack of decision-making tasks that the employees have to perform in their roles. For the most part, their jobs consist of routine, clerical, and manual work, which requires physical or on-the-job training. As employees work their way up the company ladder, they will be given more responsibility, and thus their level of authority will also increase. Different competencies will be required to adjust to the demands of the job at hand. For example, if a bookkeeper is promoted to the accounting supervisor position, his or her competencies will need to be updated. Besides maintaining their technical skill in computing, they would need to develop skills in coaching teams, scheduling work, appraising staff, and monitoring team performance.

This is also true for a finance manager who receives a promotion to become the organization's general manager. His or her new position at work would require them to be competent at measuring risk, making strategic decisions, setting goals and visions, and inspiring employees to meet performance targets. Below is a list of 12 competencies that are commonly found across many job positions and career fields. Once again, you can assess which of the 12 competencies are more appropriate for the kind of job or career field that you are looking to enter:

1. **Time Management and Priority Setting -**
   Regardless of which position you occupy within an
   organization, time management is a competency
   that is expected from everybody. Time
   management describes the ability to manage and

effectively use your time and other people's time. Candidates who have good time management tend to be self-disciplined and can manage distractions while performing a task. They are also able to meet deadlines and communicate schedules effectively with teammates.

2. **Goal Setting** - The ability to set goals and standards is usually required from candidates who are seeking managerial or supervisory positions. Managers and supervisors are expected to know how to plan activities and projects to meet the team or organization's predetermined goals successfully. They will also be required to understand how to establish goals with others and collaborate on a way forward. This will help them elicit compliance and commitment from their team members or staff and thus make the journey toward the goal more efficient.

3. **Planning and Scheduling Work** - Employees who are typically required to demonstrate this competency are either those in managerial positions or those working in production. This competency examines how well the candidate can manage and control workforce assignments and processes by utilizing people and process management techniques. It includes analyzing

complex tasks, breaking them down into manageable units or processes, using the most effective systems to plan and schedule work, and setting checkpoints or quality control measures to monitor progress.

4. **Listening and Organization** - Both listening and organization are communication competencies that are specifically helpful in dealing with people and working in teams within the organization. It assesses the candidate's ability to understand, analyze, and organize what they hear and respond to the message effectively. The breakdown of communication can prove fatalistic for an organization, especially those whose business largely involves collaborating in teams or directly communicating with customers. Strengthening this competency will require you to practice identifying inferences and assumptions, reading body language, withholding judgments that could lead to biases, and empathizing with others.

5. **Clarity of Communication** - Without clear instructions, information can be lost in translation. The ability to provide clarity in communication is a competency that is usually required from those seeking managerial or supervisory positions. Whether the information is written or verbally

communicated, these employees need to have a clear and concise way of delivering the message while reminding teams or staff members of objectives. For instance, the message would need to effectively overcome semantic or psychological barriers that may occur during interactions and maintain mutual understanding and trust.

6. **Obtaining Objective Information** - In roles involving people management, obtaining objective information is a valuable competency to have. It encourages decision-making and conflict resolution that is fair. Fairness is reached through various techniques, including asking probing questions, interviewing staff to obtain unbiased information, and using reflective questions appropriately. Obtaining objective information also requires a great deal of self-awareness and understanding of one's own biases and personal judgments. This will ensure that the outcomes are based on the evidence of facts instead of one's own beliefs about what is right or wrong.

7. **Training, Mentoring, and Delegating** - This competency is another one that is required from those who will fill people management roles. This competency helps team leaders, managers, and supervisors understand their teams or staff more

meaningfully. Understanding the group or team makes leaders influential among their subordinates. Influence is a necessary attribute to have as a leader because it helps you direct your team toward the desired company or project goals. Influence will also help leaders train and develop the people under them to perform at a higher level of excellence. The necessary skills required to train and influence a team or group successfully include coaching, advising, transferring knowledge and skills, teaching, and giving constructive feedback and criticism.

8. **Evaluating Employee Performance** - This competency describes the ability to design, test, and undertake a team or individual performance evaluation by assessing past performance and agreeing on future performance expectations. Employees with this type of competency are skilled at developing evaluation parameters, benchmarking performance, and evaluating face-to-face confrontation with staff without holding any bias.

9. **Advising and Disciplining** - Those in managerial or supervisory positions will need to know how to advise and counsel employees and fairly undertake disciplinary measures. The goal of

disciplining employees is not to punish them; rather, it is to restore their optimum performance while maintaining respect and trust. Deviations from company policies, standards, and culture can cost an organization a lot of money and time. Therefore, managers will also need to know how to impose penalties, warnings, and sanctions with firmness in appropriate circumstances.

10. **Identifying Problems and Finding Solutions** - Problem-solving is a competency that all employees will need to demonstrate regardless of their position in the organization. Problem-solving involves identifying the internal and external barriers which prevent you from achieving a particular goal or standard. It also involves applying systematic procedures to reduce or eliminate problems during the implementation of strategies and actions. Effective problem-solving involves investigating symptoms, distinguishing between various problems, assessing inputs and outcomes, assessing evidence related to the problem, and planning and recommending relevant interventions.

11. **Risk Assessment and Decision-Making** - Risk assessment and decision-making are competencies that are required from those

occupying managerial or supervisory roles. The type of decision-making required involves committing to company resources and processes that carry company-wide implications. Similarly to the problem-solving competency requirements, assessing risk and making decisions require appropriate interventions and alternatives to be identified. Every intervention must be weighed for its strengths and weaknesses and the level of risk associated. After, the best option to achieve the desired goal is selected.

12. **Thinking Analytically** - Analytical thinking is a competency required from those in managerial and supervisory positions. It involves skills such as assessing information, reaching logical conclusions, separating facts from opinions, staying clear from unwarranted assumptions, and making decisions primarily based on valid premises and sufficient information. Analytical thinking will also help managers and leaders plan for future interventions and appropriately organize company resources.

PREPARING FOR COMPETENCY-BASED INTERVIEWS

A competency-based interview differs from the traditional interview format where previous experience and qualifications were discussed while the interviewer goes through your resume. This kind of interview focuses more on testing the candidate for specific skills and personality traits that may predict their suitability for the particular job position. In these kinds of interviews, the interviewer is determined to find out whether or not you have the right experience, expertise, and cultural fit for the organization. Moreover, you are given the opportunity to demonstrate your skills and passion for the particular role.

If you have never participated in a competency-based interview before, you don't have to be anxious about preparing for one in the near future. Most of the preparation required for competency-based interviews has a lot to do with understanding the kind of questions you will be asked and knowing the correct way to answer them. Firstly, in your competency-based interview, you will notice that the questions you are asked are open-ended. This allows you room to develop in-depth responses where you describe a detailed situation or experience. As the applicant, you are expected to elaborate on a specific situation or scenario that provides evidence of your appropriateness for the job position.

Another important part of your preparation for this kind of interview involves researching the organization you are approaching.

It is important to understand what the company is about and how your position will impact the department's overall success or the organization at large. Sometimes, recruiters will stipulate the competencies that they are looking for on the job post; however, this will not be the case all of the time. When the competencies are not given, you can conduct a quick search on the typical competencies required for that position and practice answering questions that will include those competency keywords. It would also impress the interviewer if you mentioned relevant developments that have taken place in the company in recent months or years as part of your interview responses so that they know you are driven to be a part of the transformation within the organization.

The final step in your preparation involves selecting anecdotes that you can refer to during the interview process. These anecdotes refer to the stories of past professional experiences related to the job you are applying for. You can select 5 to 10 short stories, which will provide the interviewer with enough insight and evidence to form the correct assumptions about you. It is also important to assess the strength of your stories. Ask yourself, how much positive impact does this story provide? A great story includes a brief context, a problem, and an effective solution that was created at the end. If you are a college student who has not had any previous experience working in a corporate role, draw on any college experiences you have had, demonstrating your skills and competencies. The interviewer will not discount you for not having any professional experience if the job specification does not require any prior work history. However, you will be disqualified if the interviewer suspects that your stories have been falsified or exaggerated. Therefore, your anecdotes must be honest and appropriately emphasize your strengths in those situations.

The CAR and STAR Approach

There are two most popularly-used competency-based interview approaches that are recommended to candidates. Both methods will provide you with a useful framework for structuring and answering your competency-based responses. They will also encourage you to speak about your evidence of competence in a structured and coherent manner. The first approach is the CAR method, which stands for context, action, and results. In the context section, candidates are required to state the context of the situation and the problems they had to deal with. Candidates may also discuss the particular goal they were aiming to achieve and the problems that stood in achieving favorable outcomes. The second part of the response involves describing the action you took to mitigate any risks or solve the problem. In other words, you would need to state the efforts you made within the context previously given.

It is important that you present your actions in a clear and easy-to-follow way to avoid confusing the interviewer. For instance, you can describe your actions in steps from the first stage of your intervention until the last stage. After describing your actions, briefly explain why you decided to take those particular measures and the thought process behind it. You may want to describe your thought process in a systematic manner, similar to how you described your actions. Lastly, your response must include the results of your actions within the context previously given. You should only share positive outcomes with the interviewer, emphasizing how your decisions brought value to the organization or team. When describing the results of your actions, focus on being as thorough and detailed as possible. For example, in the two examples below, which one has more of an emphasis?

- " I was able to improve the efficiency in my team and got awarded for this" or;
- " I improved the train engine's efficiency by 23%, which led to a dramatic reduction in greenhouse gases. Also, 90% of my colleagues commented in a

feedback survey that they were now able to get
their work done faster."

The STAR method is a similar approach; however, it
provides the interviewer with more detail due to the addition of the "task" stage. The acronym STAR stands for situation, task, action, and results. Similarly to the context stage
in the CAR method, the situation stage requires the candidate to set the scene by describing the nature of the problem
or situation that you were faced with. Once again, your aim
here is to provide enough information to justify the steps
you take in the proceeding stages. The more detail you
provide while explaining the situation, the easier it will be
for the interviewer to see your role and contribution within
the context. The following stage requires you to highlight
the tasks you decided to perform to control, manage, plan,
or accommodate the previously stated problem.

Your tasks must also make sense in the given context. For
instance, you should always mention how the tasks you
needed to perform would help you achieve your desired goal
or outcome. Therefore, some situations may call for a few
tasks that need to be carried out. Other situations demand
more complex and systematic tasks to reach the desired goal
or outcome successfully. The following stage is where you
describe the action you took and the reason behind taking
that specific course of action. It is important to speak in the

first person, starting statements with "I" instead of "We" because you want to highlight YOUR competency and skills. Since this stage requires a lot of factual evidence, you should remember to be as thorough as possible in presenting your actions.

The final stage is where you demonstrate the results that came about after successfully performing your intervention. Similarly, with the CAR method, the results stage is where you list the positive outcomes that were achieved. If possible, you give a brief reflection on the value, lessons, and knowledge you obtained from your experience—this will also demonstrate a high level of self-awareness, which is a valuable competency to have! Ensure that you use a different situation for each competency question that the interviewer asks you because it will show them that you have experience in different areas and a diverse set of competencies. If you are writing a competency-based test or exam, make use of the word count and provide as much detail as possible. There's a reason they have given you 250 words to write your example—maximize your word count; otherwise, it may come across like you are not interested in the role that much. Lastly, make sure that you remember each anecdote clearly. Keep a copy of your practice sheet but don't take it to the interview with you! Nothing looks worse than being asked a question and rummaging around in your notes, trying to find the answer.

FOUR COMMON COMPETENCY-BASED INTERVIEW QUESTIONS AND ANSWERS

Below are examples of how to answer competency-based questions using the STAR method.

1. Give an example of a time when your communication skills made a difference in a situation.

SITUATION: While at university, I worked part-time as a training advisor and conducted training and workshops for students and staff on MS Excel, Powerpoint, and Outlook. One day, a colleague and I were delivering an advanced excel training session to a group of six students. One of the students was having trouble understanding how to apply pivot tables to the exercise we gave them. I noticed my colleague struggling to explain it in a simple and accessible way. She asked me for help.

TASK: I had to find the best way to explain the concept by adapting and tailoring my communication style and skillfully guiding the student through the steps involved in creating the correct pivot table. I also forced myself to empathize with him and understand his frustration and confusion, which reminded me of the time I was learning and struggling myself.

ACTION: Firstly, I asked the student to explain to me what he understood about pivot tables. By listening very carefully, I was able to gauge his understanding and establish what type of communication style he had. When he spoke to me, he adopted a straightforward and methodological approach, so I knew I had to do the same with him. Instead of explaining the whole concept in one go, I reasoned with him step–by–step, so that he would be able to follow the logic. I knew explaining the abstract concept may not be effective because I had observed my colleague doing that with him unsuccessfully.

RESULTS: After having guided him step-by-step, he was able to finish the exercise, and he thanked me enthusiastically for having helped him to understand and apply pivot tables. He mentioned the step-by-step approach helped him understand the logic behind the tool, and he was confident that he would be able to use pivot tables in the future.

REFLECTION: After this experience, I learned how important good communication skills are and how easy it makes getting things done.

2. Give an example of a time you worked as part of a team to complete a difficult task.

SITUATION: In my previous job, I volunteered to work with five other colleagues to produce a multi-million dollar marketing proposal. It was nearing the end of the year, and our agency was very busy working on meeting other important deadlines. Therefore, our only chance of completing this proposal was to work after hours and coordinate with each other via Skype video calls.

TASK: The task required us to work closely together, not to cause any misunderstandings—which would create further delays. I decided to create a schedule with all of the necessary components and research the team would need to fulfill. I also set up a meeting with a client representative every week to address concerns and receive valuable feedback. We followed a system whereby every week, we would assess whether we met the week's deadlines and noted the parts of the proposal that needed more work. Time was of the essence; however, we needed to collaborate to get everything done to a professional standard effectively.

ACTION: We started by reading the client brief carefully, ensuring that we understand the message the client wanted to get across. After, I decided to take the lead and allocate specific tasks based on each team member's capabilities, marketing background, and specific strong points. Once our roles were assigned, we could set a reasonable time frame that each team member would need to abide by so that the proposal would be submitted on time. Throughout our time working closely together, we supported each other and regularly communicated our concerns.

RESULT: In the end, the project was completed on time, and our client was so happy with our work that they requested for us to manage and oversee the implementation of the marketing campaign for a whole year! My manager was so impressed with my coordination and planning skills that he involved me in another project that was set to start in a few weeks.

REFLECTION: Working in a team taught me that every team member offers a valuable contribution to the overall success of a project.

3. Give an example of a time you resolved a dispute between two colleagues who were not getting along.

SITUATION: While at work, I noticed two sales representatives under my supervision had not been getting along for some time now. When I first noticed the tension between them, I took them aside individually, and we all agreed that this kind of behavior was unhealthy for the entire group's morale. Although the situation hadn't yet reached the point of impacting the company's performance or productivity, I knew that if I didn't formally intervene, the conflict could escalate.

TASK: As the team leader, I knew my responsibility was to ensure that my sales team was functioning at peak performance. Therefore, disputes between team members were not acceptable. I knew that the best way to resolve this problem was to request a meeting with both individuals and encourage open communication to find the root of the problem. I was going to mediate the discussion in a nonjudgmental and unbiased manner. My job was to listen to both individuals and clarify their message so that it was communicated effectively. My end goal was to ensure that everyone left the meeting feeling understood and supported.

ACTION: On the day of the meeting, I decided to first sit down in private with each person individually to better understand their perspective of the conflict. This helped me gather some useful information, which ultimately led me to believe that the dispute was based on a miscommunication. One team member felt that they had to work twice as hard to meet targets because of the other team member's slow work ethic. All three of us sat in a private room, and I allowed each person 10 minutes to discuss their grievances while I facilitated the conversation flow. Although there were some uncomfortable moments, both were relieved to speak openly about the situation and find a resolution.

RESULT: In the end, both team members left on good terms and agreed on the best way forward. They also spoke about ways to address conflict in the future for arguments never to reach this point again.

REFLECTION: Resolving the dispute between two of my team members showed me the devastating consequence of miscommunication between teams.

4. Can you describe a time when you have been proactive in finding a solution to a problem encountered by your customers?

SITUATION: While I was working as a sales representative at company X, I received a phone call from a customer who sounded very frustrated. They had ordered food through our online ordering app and experienced several issues in the process. The food arrived an hour late, and the customer was not notified of the time delay in our kitchen. When they opened their package, the food was cold, and they found that several items were missing.

TASK: As a sales representative, I had to investigate the matter in detail and find out where the root of the crisis began. After a few phone calls with the online operations manager and the kitchen staff, I found that the problem was due to our digital app malfunctioning. For some reason, the app could not pick up the customer's order when they first placed it. However, when it did, a few food items were missing from the order. With the problem identified, I had to reach out to the customer and explain the unfortunate ordeal.

ACTION: The customer was happy to hear that I had identified the problem. I assured him that the company would be bringing in an IT technician to conduct maintenance on our online system and ensure that a problem such as this one wouldn't happen again. After receiving approval from my superior, I then proceeded to hand the customer several coupons to use on their next purchase on our app.

RESULT: By the end of the phone call, the customer praised the company for the delicious food and drink menu that we have. Since then, I have contacted the customer on several occasions to get feedback on the quality of our app and delivery services. I am pleased to say that he has not had any complaint to make ever since resolving his first dispute.

REFLECTION: Companies can gain valuable insight from customer disputes. They can show a company where system errors lie and the most appropriate solutions to take going forward.

7

RELEVANT EXPERIENCE VERSUS
GENERAL EXPERIENCE

If you've looked for a job for a while and haven't had any luck, it is natural to feel desperate. Nonetheless, it is crucial for you to ensure that your sense of desperation doesn't leak onto your resume because this will work against you. The job market is extremely competitive, and I can guarantee you that out of the pool of applicants for any particular job vacancy, the hiring manager won't pick someone who seems too desperate for the job. Employers have many sneaky methods of spotting desperation on any given resume. For instance, desperate resumes speak subjectively about achievements instead of taking an objective approach. A candidate may describe themselves as a "world-class accountant with an exceptional eye for excellence."

On the other hand, a candidate who is not desperate won't spend all of their words exaggerating their strengths;

instead, they will try and provide the reader with as much value as possible in each section of the resume. Another method of spotting desperate applicants is assessing whether the job that was applied to matches their level of experience. If you eagerly submit your resume for positions you are not qualified for, or for those you are over-qualified, your application will reek of desperation! Sometimes job seekers mistakenly apply for the wrong job because they fail to research what exactly the position entails. You might see the job title as "support" at the end and assume it is similar to the supportive role that you have performed in the past.

Other job seekers are ready to pivot into a new career field, so they apply for slightly different jobs from what they are used to doing. In this case, adding a cover letter to your resume explaining why you are interested in making this career shift will help hiring managers understand your stance a lot better. Finally, desperate job seekers are easily spotted because they tend to divulge their lengthy career history on several pages of their resume. They will include every school that they attended since pre-school, their personal information (including identity number), and every small detail about their experience at each company. The most attractive kinds of resumes are short, full of value, and, most importantly, are focused specifically on highlighting career milestones and achievements fitting to the specific company and position they are applying for.

CREATING AN ATTRACTIVE RESUME

A one-size-fits-all approach to create a resume won't help you much during your job search. There are too many negative connotations that come to mind when I think of generic resumes. For the most part, it gives hiring managers the wrong impression of you as a talented job seeker; therefore, you must avoid implementing a "copy and send" approach in distributing your cover letter and resume. Instead, it would be helpful for you to learn how to create an attractive resume. Ironically, attractive resumes have very little to do with the aesthetic appeal of your document. The attractiveness of a resume has a lot to do with how useful it is to the reader. Take a moment and think about the type of online articles you are attracted to. Most of the time, these articles aren't necessarily the prettiest (if you even noticed), but they do offer a load of value!

Adding value to your resume requires you to customize each one you send specifically for the role and company you are applying to. It would be very embarrassing if your generic resume or cover letter mentioned the name of another company rather than the company you were sending it to. While it's an editing error, it also shows a lack of concern for your professional brand and how your overall first impression comes across. The best way to impress your future employer is by tailoring your resume to match the particular position you are applying for and provide evidence that shows you would be the perfect addition to their company. To do this, you would need to research the company and find ways to incorporate aspects of their culture, vision, and direction as an organization. Even though tailoring your resume in this manner will take you a lot longer than sending a generic document, it will create a positive impression about you. Sending a targeted resume is the difference between a hiring manager thinking, "She's nice" and "I need her to start on Monday!" after having a look through your resume.

It is also useful to tailor your resume because nowadays, companies use software to process incoming applications before the "targeted" ones reach the hiring manager. The software used is known as applicant tracking systems (ATS), and they are used by recruiters to weed out inappropriate applications. The software will scan an application and search for keywords that are related to the particular job position. The resumes that do not have these relevant keywords will immediately become disqualified. In other words, when a job seeker's application is not customized to the specific role that they are applying for, the chances of their resume reaching the hiring manager are very slim. Therefore, when you create your resume, ensure that your document is keyword-friendly, including common language that someone qualified for that role would use. Alternatively, you can structure your resume based on the job description. The job description includes many relevant keywords and essential skills that the hiring manager will look for.

Finally, an attractive resume includes relevant work experience and skills. Many people use their resumes to boast about their accolades and the wonderful companies they have worked for in the past. Unfortunately, recruiters won't care very much about your elaborate career history—all they care about is whether or not you are the perfect fit for their organization. Moreover, when you list every small and large skill that you have acquired since high school, your most profitable skills will go unnoticed or appear insignificant on the list. As much as it is tempting to include a full timeline of your career, it may not always play to your advantage. From your long list of skills and lengthy career history, focus your attention on those aspects that your future employer will be interested to see. You can use the job description as a benchmark to assess the relevant work experience, skills, and achievements your future employer would be thrilled to see. Every other small detail about your career history can be discussed over coffee.

THE UNWRITTEN REQUIREMENTS

The job description is not a comprehensive summary of everything the hiring manager is looking for from a candidate. When an HR executive drafts the job specifications for a particular position, they are restricted regarding the level of detail they can provide. As knowledgeable as the HR executive is on all job positions in the company, they aren't aware of the daily activities happening within a department or teams. Therefore, there could be many aspects of the job that are not mentioned in the advertised job descriptions. If HR doesn't completely know what the job entails or the perfect candidate to fill the role, the hiring manager should surely know what they are looking for, right? Well, in most cases, hiring managers don't know what they are looking for, either!

Consider the events that had to have occurred for the position to be vacant.

- The person who was acting in that role was promoted and thus had to fill another position.
- The person who was acting in that role quit and a replacement had to be found.
- The company fired the person, and thus someone else had to be found.

- The role is a new position that needs someone to fill.

In all of these scenarios listed above, the hiring manager was forced to establish a candidate criteria that they believed was necessary for the work to be carried out successfully. The only problem is that the hiring manager, similarly with the HR executive, finds it difficult to identify the soft skills that are needed for the role. For instance, it isn't easy for a hiring manager to describe what personality they are looking for in the pool of candidates waiting to be interviewed. It is also not easy for the hiring manager to determine the aptitude that a candidate must have to learn in the organization's work environment. Therefore, how do hiring managers find "the one?" The perfect candidate for the role is typically identified through a series of screenings, which gives the hiring manager a better idea of the kind of candidate they are looking for.

For example, have you ever had an interview and were told that your interview went very well, only for the company to tell you that they decided to choose another candidate? However, a few days after your interview, you notice that the job post is back on the Internet, but this time, there has been an adjustment regarding job specifications. If you can relate with this experience, it means that you were, unfortunately, part of a job description fine-tuning process where the hiring manager was using the interview with you to determine what exactly they were and were not looking for in a perfect candidate. There is no way for you to avoid being a victim of this fine-tuning process because chances are you won't even know that you are a part of it. Nevertheless, there is a way for you to stay in the running for a job during the fine-tuning process.

The solution is to leave a lasting impression during your interview. How can you do this? By boldly expressing your personality and aptitude. If you are able to personally connect with a hiring manager and capture their attention throughout the interviewing process, you could leave a strong enough impression that makes them adjust the job description in your favor! Instead of worrying about how well your resume markets your capabilities or the kind of questions you will be asked during the interview, focus instead on establishing a relationship with the hiring manager from the moment you two meet. Being likable is the unwritten requirement that you will never see listed as one of the prerequisites for landing the job; however, your likeability is all that counts during the interview.

THE SECRET INGREDIENTS TO MAKING YOUR RESUME STAND OUT

You may be the most skilled person in your friend group, class, or family; however, when your resume is stacked in between 250 other applications to be considered, your awesomeness is hidden. Therefore, it is important to draft your resume with one specific goal: the hiring manager should want to read your resume from top to bottom at least twice! This is an ambitious goal to have, but it is possible to achieve when you have an understanding of the secret ingredients that must be included in your resume. Firstly, your resume must include both hard and soft skills. Hard skills are related to the technical knowledge and training you have acquired for a particular job position. They are often acquired through your educational career and training. For example, if you have worked for a retail store, you may know how to use a point-of-sale system, or if you have taken a crash course in accounting, you will be familiar with Microsoft Excel.

On the other hand, soft skills include personality traits and behaviors that have influenced how you work on your own and with others in an organization. Typically, we spend our whole lives developing soft skills because they are primarily learned from our personal or professional experiences. These skills become advantageous when you have to manage your time wisely, communicate effectively with team members, or healthily resolve conflict. A candidate who is applying for an HR role will be assessed more critically on their soft skills than their hard skills. A large part of their work will require them to empathize with staff members, adopt an open-mind, and effectively resolve disputes.

The second ingredient for making your resume stand out from the rest is to create well-structured work experience descriptions. This is perhaps the most difficult component involved in designing a resume. Each description explaining your work history, achievements, or extracurricular activities should be clear and descriptive (without being too wordy). You want the hiring manager to know what your responsibilities were in your previous jobs and the skills you have developed. Therefore, consider describing your responsibilities in brief statements full of strong verbs. You don't have to list all of the skills you acquired on the job but only those that will highlight your strengths as they relate to the job you are applying for. Whenever it is appropriate, you should always quantify your achievements and responsibilities. For example, this would mean using numbers, currency values, and percentages to emphasize the value that was created. Below are examples of how much power statements have when quantities have been added:

- "Increased monthly sales by 50%."

- "Managed and mentored 20 employees."
- "Processed daily receipts totaling £2,000."

TIPS TO GET THE HIRING MANAGER TO READ YOUR ENTIRE RESUME

It is a known fact that hiring managers won't read every application that is sent to them. Some hiring managers have been known to use the "6-second rule," where they dedicate 6 seconds to skim through the resume and see whether the candidate is what they are looking for. This forces job seekers to be intentional when creating their resumes to grab the hiring manager's attention from the beginning. Besides the 6-second rule, there is a general method that some hiring managers implement when opening job applications. Understanding how hiring managers interpret your resume will help you design your resume in a way that stands out!

When a hiring manager opens your resume for the first time, they will make a split-second judgment about your overall presentation. Their eyes will focus on the contact information provided and the location of the candidate. Location on its own can be a make-or-break factor, especially for positions where candidates are expected to be familiar with the company's community. For job seekers who are willing to locate to a different town for work must clearly state this in their cover letter so that their resume is not quickly dismissed. When a hiring manager can spend less time finding your personal information, they will have more time to look through the rest of your resume. Therefore, make sure that your personal information is bold and centered to make the hiring manager's job a lot easier.

The second step is usually for the hiring manager to quickly assess the resume's length and the density of the information provided. Resumes that are longer than two pages and crammed with wall-to-wall text were an immediate turnoff. Resumes are meant to be an introductory document showing the hiring manager that you are worth contacting for more screening. Therefore, avoid treating your resume as though it is your only chance to make a good impression. Instead, select the most valuable information about your career to add to your resume. Another major red flag for hiring managers is strange design techniques that make it difficult to piece together who the candidate is. I understand that everybody wants to have the most visually-appealing resume that stands out; however, sometimes, the visual appeal can be distracting or simply unprofessional. If you insist on using functional resume templates (the latest trend I must add), it would be wise for you to design it to draw a clear link between your transferable skills and the requirements listed on the job post.

After skimming through the resume, hiring managers tend to zero-in on the top third of the resume. This section is known as the prime real estate of all resumes. This is because many hiring managers won't have enough time to read through every page, and thus, this top third section usually provides them with enough information to either rule you out or rule in your favor. Therefore, you must ensure that your top third section is full of rich keywords and makes a meaningful impact. Remember your X-Factor? This is where it comes out. Emphasize your value, add to the company, and draw as many similarities between what your brand and the company requires. If you are going to add a brief career summary, make sure that every word makes a valuable contribution to marketing yourself and your skills. Remember that being too wordy can make you look desperate; thus, every word you decide to put on your resume must be useful.

If you have managed to keep the hiring manager's attention for this long, they will proceed to your qualifications section. Before reading this section in-depth, hiring managers will check to see if you are a fit for the company based on your education, training, certifications, licenses, and previous job titles. Therefore, make sure that these elements stand out and are easy to read. If you are still in the process of completing your degree or certification, you should add it to your resume and list the date that you expect to complete it by. Some hiring managers will agree to give you a job with the expectation that you will have completed your degree or training by the listed date. After having a look at your qualifications, a hiring manager will want to see your accomplishments. Many job seekers believe that listing accomplishments is a nice-to-have section; however, achievements are an important marketing tool.

Accomplishments should always be written in bullet points because it is much easier to read. The kinds of accomplishments that a hiring manager would find impressive include ways that you have helped other companies save money, ways you have helped to repair office relationships, or how you have participated in your community outside of the work environment. Ensure that many of your accomplishments are work-related and clearly show how these contributions have helped companies reach their bottom-line. High-impact accomplishments are so enticing to hiring managers to the extent that, in some cases, these accomplishments will determine the potential salary that they are willing to offer you!

These are only some of the tips for keeping the hiring manager's attention for longer than 6-seconds. When you design your resume with this information in mind, you will have an attractive resume. You must also consider that the hiring team is not exactly on your side throughout the application screening process. They have the enormous job of sorting through hundreds of resumes and ruling out as many as they can. They are looking for only the best candidates who will make it through to the next round of screening for a more in-depth review. Therefore, with this in mind, make sure that your resume does not include any red flags, grammar or spelling mistakes, or missing information. The goal of sending your resume is to secure the next round of job screening and not necessarily to land a job just yet. Remember that you are a professional brand trying to convince another brand to form a partnership with you.

8

JOB HUNTING IN DIFFICULT TIMES
AND FUTURE JOB MARKET TRENDS

Many workers may be forced to start looking for a new job as redundancies are made and entire sectors evolve. The destabilizing effects of the global issues we have been presented in recent years—such as global warming, economic recessions, and recently, the coronavirus—have created job insecurity like never before. With companies having to shut down indefinitely and others having to reduce their number of staff, many industries are in a vulnerable situation, and the economy's future outcomes are unknown. Although sometimes it's too early to predict how the jobs market will evolve due to changes in the economy, or a global pandemic, we can be confident in saying that both candidates and clients will experience extremely challenging conditions. During unprecedented times like this, job seekers are unsure when the next big natural disaster or health scare will hit. Therefore, it is important for them to have an understanding of how unforeseen changes to their environment can impact their job search and build strategies to combat this. For instance, job seekers would need to start thinking about how to make the most of their transferable skills and knowing how to stand out in a crowded field.

If you've previously worked in a sector that has been forced to close due to the coronavirus, for example, do you have any experience you can take into new areas? Those in hospitality may have a lot of experience in customer care, so they would need to ask themselves, "Can my skill be moved into a sales role?" If you've specialized in events management, could you move into a similar area of marketing or PR? Could you examine your project management and organizational skills and try something new in a different sector? For example, many IT or SEO organizations may require dedicated account managers to cope with multiple clients or projects. Your time is precious during these precarious times, and therefore you need to use your time to upskill yourself in something which allows flexibility to work from home. Technology-based jobs are and will always be in high demand. Use this knowledge to your advantage and learn to code or work for free and build your portfolio.

In other words, your goal should be to gain professional qualifications and experience in case anything does end up affecting your job security. Your transferable skills are an asset to you that allows you to use the same knowledge that you have gained in one role to work in another one. For example, if you are an event manager—and currently struggling with the job market due to tough times—use this time to train up on some PRINCE2 qualifications, so you can transfer into a project management role, as you already have a lot of the transferable skills needed for that role. Another tip is to remember to emphasize your soft skills in the application form, as these also mean a lot. Perhaps you're incredibly good with people and have an exceptional track record in customer service, or maybe you're strong at multitasking and handling multiple projects simultaneously. Include these skills on your resume because hiring managers may be looking for candidates with rich, soft skills.

Even during tough times, don't forget to ensure you read the job description properly and only apply for jobs you are suitable for. If times are really bad, like during the COVID-19 pandemic, prepare yourself to do interviews online. Make sure that you look professional, ask for an itinerary in advance, sort out any technical issues that could cause problems for you and the employer, and prepare your meeting room in a well-lit area. In the future, the job market may look a lot different from how it looks now. Many administration, manual, and retail jobs will disappear and be replaced by robots or technology. Therefore, you need to prioritize upskilling yourself, focusing particularly on building or enhancing those skills with longevity.

THE FUTURE OF WORK

The work environment has begun changing. New technologies, digitization of work functions, and automation have replaced thousands of jobs and completely changed how many industries are sustained. The nature of jobs is also changing, with more temporary contracts, gigs, and remote work being favored over traditional permanent contracts. While many jobs are going to be lost, many will be created. One thing that none of us can deny is that every job will be tested for its appropriateness in this new global work landscape. The mark of the new decade has brought along unexpected shifts in the workforce, quicker than any of us would have imagined. Those who had never previously considered a home office are now making arrangements to create one as office parks, and buildings have closed down. Boardroom meetings that were previously held on the premises are now being taken via Zoom conference calls, connecting people from anywhere in the world.

Some of the changes that you see taking shape today began gradually before the wake of COVID-19—however, this global health crisis has significantly accelerated the transformation in how we work. The agenda to digitize work has been an ongoing process, with organizations finding ways to conduct most of their operations on digital platforms and connect outside of the office. While many assume that some of these new changes are only here temporarily or due to global lockdowns, most of them are here to stay. There are four major shifts which are expected to become more prominent in the years to come:

1. **Remote Jobs** - The future of work post-COVID looks remote. Many companies have seen how effective collaborations online have been through the work-from-home measures taken during the pandemic. Working from home is now the new normal for many organizations. Many employees are also enjoying the benefits that working remotely offers. For instance, a recent study showed that 83% of employees (both those who worked remotely and on-site) said that a remote work opportunity would make them feel more fulfilled with their work (*4 Trends That Are Shaping the Future of Work*, 2020). Employee satisfaction leads to increased productivity, and therefore remote work proves to be a win-win situation for both employer and employee. With

more collaborative social networking platforms emerging, remote work is said to offer the same work style that employees were used to in a physical office.

2. **Digital Transformation** - It's no secret that technology is perhaps the most influential factor (apart from the economy) regarding how we work. As newer technologies are invented and adopted in the world of work, the workforce structure will inevitably change. More companies have already started preparing their workforce to adopt a digital mindset where most processes are carried out digitally, in a more efficient and cost-saving way. For the time being, the kind of digital transformation that companies are implementing has less to do with replacing staff members with robots but more focused on solving team and company problems with technology and increasing productivity. For instance, software such as Microsoft Teams, Slack and Google Drive are making communication between teams and individuals smoother and decreasing the friction that tends to occur in the workplace.

3. **The Takeover of Millennials** - With the rise of technology, organizations are searching for people who will be able to work with digital

technology comfortably. Millennials describe a generation of young people who were born just before and during the technological boom. When these tech-savvy professionals complete their education, they are prepared for the digital transformation taking place within the job market. Older staff are slowly being phased out of the professional workforce. Younger professionals are in high demand, especially in leadership positions, due to their forward-thinking and goal-oriented mind. With this transformation in leadership, we are beginning to see a modern type of leader emerging who values innovation and value learning instead of routine work or perfectionism.

4. **The Scalable Workforce** - As more changes occur in the economic and company landscape, more companies are adjusting their structures and the size of their workforce. More companies are cutting down on permanent staff and teams because a scalable workforce is seen as being more flexible, especially during an unexpected economic downturn. The workforce is adjusted as needed to accommodate financial and industry fluctuations. Full-time employees are seen as being costly. This is because a full-time position comes with extra benefits, such as contributions toward a pension

fund, medical benefits and bonuses. Thus, many companies are now outsourcing business functions, hiring contractual staff, or finding once-off freelancers to perform specific business tasks. In recent years, websites offering expert talent for business projects or recurring tasks have been on the rise. Some of these websites include Fiverr, Assemble, and Upwork.

THE FUTURE OF SKILLS

In 10 years, the chances of working in a job that doesn't yet exist are significantly high. As the world of work transforms rapidly, job seekers need to think about how they can start preparing for future jobs that may or may not exist. Of course, you can't predict how your professional life will look like in the future and which skills will be valuable or not; however, there are a few predictable skills that you will need to develop to prepare for the new wave of jobs in the future:

1. **Cognitive Flexibility** - The creation and adoption of new technologies will require you to build competencies to handle the opportunities and challenges that come with technology. For example, are you able to adapt to change and conceptualize ideas all at the same time? Suppose your answer

was yes (which would be highly impressive). In that case, you are already demonstrating advanced multi-tasking abilities that will be necessary in the future when your job requires you to organize and process large amounts of information all at once.

2. **Computational Thinking** - Technology is constantly evolving, and for you to survive in the future job market, your digital skills will need to improve continuously. It's not enough to know how to create a PowerPoint presentation because nowadays, presentations are created and hosted on cloud servers. I understand that it may feel like you are bombarded with new digital buzzwords at times, but these buzzwords point to trends that are here to stay. For example, the more digitally literate you are, the more prepared you will be to integrate or work with technologies like artificial intelligence, the Internet of Things, 3-D printing, and machine learning, to name a few. Studying short courses in these technologies will help increase your digital skills and significantly raise your technical acumen in these emerging technological fields.

3. **Decision-Making** - Decision-making is already a valuable competency to have in the current job market. However, in the future, you will be

competing with robots and machines in making the best decision for the company. Who will outsmart who? Fortunately for you, as intelligent as robots are in making calculations and diagnosing problems, they cannot assess the data analytics subjective nature. Therefore, even in this fourth industrial revolution that we are entering, companies will still rely on people like you to subjectively interpret numbers and assess their significance to the company.

4. **Emotional and Social Intelligence** - Similarly to the point made above, emotional and social intelligence is something that a machine cannot learn for now. These are intrinsically human capabilities that will keep the human workforce in demand, even during technological transformation. There are some industries where emotional and social intelligence is extremely important. For instance, healthcare workers will continue to be in demand as populations increase and healthcare professionals are needed. Other jobs that will continue to depend on human insight and touch include psychology, social work, law, sales, and marketing. If you are in a career that will continue to depend on human interaction, it would be important for you to continue cultivating empathy,

improving your communication skills, and learning how to collaborate effectively with others.

5. **An Innovative Mindset** - Another advantage that human beings have over robots is that we can hone in on our creative minds. Machines are programmed to think in certain ways, but who programs the human mind? Think back to the beginning of your career and the amount of knowledge and skills that you had. I am sure it was a fraction of the knowledge and skills that you have now. Along your career journey, your mind has expanded to incorporate a wealth of wisdom that you use to navigate your career path today. This ability to seek, discover, and learn is a human gift. Depending on what you choose to focus your mind on today, you would have adopted a new way of thinking and living 10 years from now. Applying your natural creativity to your work will help you think out of the box regarding how far you can go in your career and the amount of new knowledge you can acquire. A machine cannot replicate your natural creativity, and therefore it will always be an asset in your personal and professional life.

5 FUTURE EMPLOYMENT TRENDS

With global unemployment on the incline, the competition for jobs has become increasingly tight. Companies that desire to stay relevant in the recruitment environment are ditching the old job roles and workforce structures that used to work in previous years. Instead, these companies are thinking out of the box when it comes to what constitutes employment. Traditional work concepts are being gradually replaced with new job specifications and titles that are influenced by advances in technology. Job seekers are eager to find out the current and future trends of hiring talent to change their strategies and adapt to the new normal.

1. **The Rise of Artificial Intelligence** - Artificial intelligence (AI) has increased in popularity because of the growing need for operational efficiency within companies. Artificial intelligence is seen as a strategic resource to organizations, helping them analyze large quantities of data, which is useful in making critical company decisions. This technology is also useful in helping HR make hiring decisions. For instance, AI can help a recruiter create search keywords for the best candidate match. It can help review and filter through candidate resumes and find those who are a perfect fit for the company,

and it can also predict a candidate's performance on the job and how long they are likely to stay in the company. All of this information is obtained from complex algorithms, contextual analysis, as well as image recognition. The level of precision attainable when using AI is unmatched and less prone to error than human analysis.

2. **Agile Team Structures** - The idea of full-time work is no longer as influential as it was many years ago. Nowadays, work is flexible, meaning that companies are open to hiring independent contractors, consultants, or outsourcing partners in the expanding "gig" economy. Companies can access highly-skilled people for projects or campaigns without having to hire them full-time. This is advantageous to the company because it allows it to cope with industry and market-related challenges while capitalizing on the new skills and talent of an on-demand workforce.

3. **The Emphasis on Workforce Diversity** - As companies become more tech-savvy, they are increasingly finding the need to become more socially conscious. It has taken many years for organizations to prioritize the diversity agenda within their workforce. A diverse workforce benefits the organization because it welcomes

employees with a broader perspective and experience. This adds to the organization's culture by including employees with diverse backgrounds, education, and skills. Diversity within an organization begins in the recruitment process by removing inherent hiring biases and widening the net to allow new faces, voices, and talent to bring value to an organization.

4. **The Power of an Employer Brand** - Companies are increasingly seeing the need to create a reputable brand for themselves to remain competitive in the corporate environment. One of the pressures companies experience comes directly from job seekers. Talented job seekers who are in high-demand are going to choose the most reputable companies to work for. They tend to select companies that complete sizable and strategic projects to earn valuable work experience. As a result of the candidates' preferences, companies are working toward marketing themselves to appeal to job seekers and the experience they are looking for. For instance, a company may promote its transparent and fair work environment, while another may promote the number of growth opportunities available in the company.

5. **Shifting the Recruitment Process to Social**

Media - Many years ago, you would barely find a company with a social media account. Social media was seen as being too informal for business operations. Nowadays, businesses are using social media not only to communicate with customers but to recruit new talent. Companies are learning that it is possible to scout for the best talent on social media by targeting job seekers on the most relevant social media channels. Companies are forced to provide tailored content to fit a specific social media platform and appeal to a candidate's perceived job-related desires. Sometimes, the simple act of including branded social media content like a video of the company's work culture can attract interested job seekers.

CONCLUSION

The process of finding a job is undoubtedly stressful. The stress experienced from this demanding process is further heightened by the growing pressures to earn a livelihood and become financially independent. Whether you are fresh out of college or entering your third career shift, finding a job is a puzzling process that isn't easy to decode. I believe that most of the misfortune that you have experienced during this process resulted from using old formulas and strategies for finding a stable job. In previous years, companies were satisfied with a simple cover letter and resume to make their hiring decisions. Nowadays, a cover letter and a resume will barely get you to the next round of the recruitment process. So, what has changed?

Companies, just like human beings, react to the changes that are presented in their environment. When the economic environment is prosperous, for example, a company will thrive and achieve great success. However, when the economic environment has been negatively impacted by other political and social factors, companies are also hit hard. In an attempt to survive, executives are forced to adapt. Therefore, the change that we are witnessing in the job hunting process is due to companies adapting to a new world and the new challenges it presents. One of the consequences of the global economic turmoil has been a rise in unemployment. Simply put, companies cannot afford to sustain a large workforce anymore. They have had to rely on technology to make functions more efficient so that fewer employees are needed. Another consequence of the economic downturn has been the rise in competition for vacant jobs.

No one disputes that our colleges and workplaces are full of talented individuals. There is so much talent within company structures that hiring managers are not necessarily looking for talent anymore. Instead, they are looking for candidates who can demonstrate value. Throughout this book, I spoke about X-Factor, and if there is anything you retain from this book, let this be something worth remembering. Remember that the best way to make a hiring manager interested in hiring you as opposed to hiring someone else lies in you displaying your X-Factor. It will show your future employer that you are not merely desiring to work for the organization due to needing a job but also because you have a gift or skill that could potentially help them become more productive or make more money. Therefore, the commodity that we find being bought and sold in interview rooms is value and not necessarily qualifications.

The good news is that you have been cultivating your value for many years. Through the course of your studies, you have had the chance to discover your passions and set a career vision. This planning has allowed you to identify your strengths and weaknesses and areas where you need to improve. This level of self-awareness and rich understanding of who you are and what you have to offer is what hiring managers will want to see in your resume. Don't be shy to express your unique attributes and the hard work you have invested in building your professional brand. Marketing yourself to your future employer is not a desperate attempt; instead, it demonstrates the impact that you have made in your career thus far.

As I have shown to you in this book, the world of the workforce is transforming. You can be one of the people who benefit from this transformation by ensuring that you have the skills and training that will be in-demand in a few years. Expose yourself to the innovative technologies that are changing industries and learn about how they operate.

Regularly attend industry events and conferences where new trends, processes, and training are discussed. These events can also become an excellent way for you to rub shoulders with change-makers in various sectors. As a job seeker in this COVID era, you have an opportunity to position yourself in the right industry, having the right skills, at the right time. Recognize that you are sitting in the power seat, and therefore you should make strategic decisions regarding which company you want to work for. Look at the various benefits, criteria, and implications of taking on certain job roles or accepting a specific salary. Carry this book with you and make references to it whenever you feel "stuck" or need some extra motivation to continue on your search. You can also send a copy of this book to a friend or colleague as a gift, giving them access to the same knowledge and tips you have learned about the job market.

I hope that you can use this book as a manual throughout your job hunting process. All of the knowledge and truth that I have shared with you has helped me climb the corporate ladder and live a successful life, one that I have always desired. I could not have reached these heights of success without adjusting my mentality about the job market and having a sober outlook on what it would take to achieve my career goals within a specific time. I found that the secret to implementing some of these powerful strategies lies in opening your mind to different possibilities and getting out of your comfort zone. Perhaps you haven't seen any new changes primarily because you have been doing the same thing repeatedly for many months. Commit to switching things up and trying out new strategies to find your ideal job. Have fun recreating your professional image, networking, and making the first contact with hiring managers. You have absolutely nothing to lose but a world of good to gain. Your contribution to the corporate world is significant, and it deserves to be seen and experienced by the most reputable companies in your industry. You have so much value to share with your future place of work and with your community. Get up, get dressed, and let the world see your light! I wish you all the best in your professional endeavors!

Just for you

A FREE GIFT FOR OUR READERS!

A list of 5 common mistakes people make whilst searching for a job and info on how you can overcome them!
Visit this link:

WWW.Z-LAWSON.COM

For further discussion and support, join our community of advisors and friends on

www.facebook.com/groups/jobsearchadviceforum

Made in United States
North Haven, CT
22 June 2025

70030993R00090